ESSENTIALS OF

# Thematic Analysis

# Essentials of Qualitative Methods Series

ESSENTIALS OF

# Thematic Analysis

Gareth Terry
Nikki Hayfield

 **AMERICAN PSYCHOLOGICAL ASSOCIATION**

Published by
American Psychological Association
750 First Street, NE
Washington, DC 20002
https://www.apa.org

Order Department
https://www.apa.org/pubs/books
order@apa.org

In the U.K., Europe, Africa, and the Middle East, copies may be ordered from Eurospan
https://www.eurospanbookstore.com/apa
info@eurospangroup.com

Typeset in Charter and Interstate by Circle Graphics, Inc., Reisterstown, MD

Printer: Gasch Printing, Odenton, MD
Cover Designer: Anne C. Kerns, Anne Likes Red, Inc., Silver Spring, MD

**Library of Congress Cataloging-in-Publication Data**

Names: Terry, Gareth, author. | Hayfield, Nikki, author.
Title: Essentials of thematic analysis / Gareth Terry and Nikki Hayfield.
Description: Washington, DC : American Psychological Association, [2021] |
  Series: Essentials of qualitative methods | Includes bibliographical
  references and index.
Identifiers: LCCN 2020051939 (print) | LCCN 2020051940 (ebook) |
  ISBN 9781433835575 (paperback) | ISBN 9781433835582 (ebook)
Subjects: LCSH: Qualitative research—Methodology. | Social sciences—
  Research—Methodology.
Classification: LCC H62 .T364 2021 (print) | LCC H62 (ebook) |
  DDC 300.72/1—dc23
LC record available at https://lccn.loc.gov/2020051939
LC ebook record available at https://lccn.loc.gov/2020051940

https://doi.org/10.1037/0000238-000

*Printed in the United States of America*

10 9 8 7 6 5 4

# Contents

# Series Foreword

Qualitative approaches have become accepted and indeed embraced as empirical methods within the social sciences, as scholars have realized that many of the phenomena in which we are interested are complex and require deep inner reflection and equally penetrating examination. Quantitative approaches often cannot capture such phenomena well through their standard methods (e.g., self-report measures), so qualitative designs using interviews and other in-depth data-gathering procedures offer exciting, nimble, and useful research approaches.

Indeed, the number and variety of qualitative approaches that have been developed is remarkable. We remember Bill Stiles saying (quoting Chairman Mao) at one meeting about methods, "Let a hundred flowers bloom," indicating that there are many appropriate methods for addressing research questions. In this series, we celebrate this diversity (hence, the cover design of flowers).

The question for many of us, though, has been how to decide among approaches and how to learn the different methods. Many prior descriptions of the various qualitative methods have not provided clear enough descriptions of the methods, making it difficult for novice researchers to learn how to use them. Thus, those interested in learning about and pursuing qualitative research need crisp and thorough descriptions of these approaches, with lots of examples to illustrate the method so that readers can grasp how to use the methods.

The purpose of this series of books, then, is to present a range of qualitative approaches that seemed most exciting and illustrative of the range of methods appropriate for social science research. We asked leading experts in qualitative methods to contribute to the series, and we were delighted that they accepted our invitation. Through this series, readers have the opportunity to learn qualitative research methods from those who developed the methods and/or who have been using them successfully for years.

We asked the authors of each book to provide context for the method, including a rationale, situating the method within the qualitative tradition, describing the method's philosophical and epistemological background, and noting the key features of the method. We then asked them to describe in detail the steps of the method, including the research team, sampling, biases and expectations, data collection, data analysis, and variations on the method. We also asked authors to provide tips for the research process and for writing a manuscript emerging from a study that used the method. Finally, we asked authors to reflect on the methodological integrity of the approach, along with the benefits and limitations of the particular method.

This series of books can be used in several different ways. Instructors teaching courses in qualitative research could use the whole series, presenting one method at a time to expose students to a range of qualitative methods. Alternatively, instructors could choose to focus on just a few approaches, as depicted in specific books, supplementing the books with examples from studies that have been published using the approaches, and providing experiential exercises to help students get started using the approaches.

Terry and Hayfield's book on a reflexive approach to thematic analysis provides a clear description of how to construct "situated truth" from qualitative data. The authors emphasize that this approach is a method (i.e., a flexible tool to fit the needs of a specific project) rather than a methodology (i.e., including a theoretical framework). They celebrate the idea of flexibility, subjectivity, and going beyond mere summaries of the data to deep understandings of the underlying structures. The method requires extensive engagement with the data and consistent efforts to check and think about analytic understandings. The book is designed for both beginners and experts, bringing the method to life with extensive tips, figures, and exhibits.

—*Clara E. Hill and Sarah Knox*

ESSENTIALS OF
# Thematic Analysis

# 1 CONCEPTUAL FOUNDATIONS OF THEMATIC ANALYSIS

Over the last decade, thematic analysis (TA) has become an increasingly popular way of engaging with qualitative data. TA is highly cited as an analytic method of choice for many, not only within psychology but also across a wide range of disciplines (Joffe, 2012; Terry et al., 2017). Researchers positioned within most theoretical frameworks can use TA to do justice to the piles of interview or focus group transcripts, qualitative survey responses, or other qualitative data they have generated. TA is a flexible analytical method that enables the researcher to construct themes—meaning-based patterns—to report their interpretation of a qualitative data set. It has proven utility for novice and experienced researchers alike, as can be seen in the vast numbers of theses, dissertations, papers, and reports that cite one version of TA or another as their primary analytic method. Among those who have been convinced of its merits, it is viewed as a rigorous, powerful, and yet "straightforward" way of engaging with qualitative data.

Despite the newness of the method's explosion in use, versions of TA have been around a long time. These versions were often just not described as TA at all, were poorly described, or were aligned with particular methodologies and thus already wedded to a theoretical framework. Consequently, over

15 years ago, Braun and Clarke (2006) argued that TA was taken for granted, commonly deployed, and yet poorly described and delineated. The landscape has changed, though. Braun and Clarke's 2006 paper has now been cited many thousands of times on Google Scholar, and alongside other writing about TA, there is a now a developing corpus of work that helps clarify the various ways TA can be used and understood (e.g., Braun & Clarke, 2012, 2019a; Braun et al., 2015, 2018, 2019; Clarke et al., 2015; Terry & Hayfield, 2020; Terry et al., 2017).

What has become clear through the work of Braun, Clarke, and their colleagues is that there is more than one expression of TA, something we discuss in more detail later in this chapter and in Chapter 6. Although Braun and Clarke's (2006) seminal paper is popular, it speaks about a particular type of TA—what they have since referred to as *reflexive* TA (Braun & Clarke, 2019a; Braun et al., 2018, 2019). Central to reflexive TA is the idea of *reflexivity*, or the importance of the researcher's interpretation of the data. Within reflexive TA, analysis occurs because of, rather than despite, the researcher's subjectivity—their values, backgrounds, decisions, and interests. In contrast to methods that attempt to create objective "distance" because of concerns about bias, reflexive TA is premised on the engagement of the researcher with their data, guided by their research question and theoretical orientations. In this text, we aim to contribute to increasing clarity regarding the shape and utility of reflexive TA.

Although TA more generally is no longer "poorly demarcated" (Braun & Clarke, 2006, p. 77), there is still work needed to ensure that the use of reflexive TA, and its ongoing evolution, continue to reflect its fundamental core values: (a) theoretical flexibility; (b) procedural focus on a systematic, ever-increasing, and rigorous engagement with data; (c) emphasis on the reflexive contribution of the researcher; and (d) framing of "themes" as multi-faceted, conceptual, meaning-based patterns. We keep returning to these core values throughout this book because they are central to the doing of reflexive TA. However, along with Virginia Braun and Victoria Clarke, we do not view this method as strictly following a recipe or a set of "rules" (Braun et al., 2019). Reflexive TA is simply one way of thematizing qualitative data that we think has considerable value in the wider qualitative research conversation.

We draw on almost 30 years of combined experience to help shape this text and its focus. We were both students of Virginia Braun (Gareth) and Victoria Clarke (Nikki), directly benefiting from their input into our work and, more recently, collaborating with them on writing about reflexive TA. We have both worked extensively to support people using TA, teaching the approach through workshops, formal lectures, tutoring, one-to-one problem solving, and informal conversations. We have used it in our published work and supported others' use of it in theirs. We hope that this text acts to supplement this ongoing support of people who are interested in TA—particularly its reflexive expression. We intend this text to give you a starting point, to act as a guide, but we will continually highlight that all research design comes with history, context, and decades of academic conversation and writing. Therefore, we recommend reading widely, and we point you in the direction of texts that have helped our research journeys, to some of the corpus of writing we referred to earlier in the chapter, and to exemplar studies listed in the Appendix.

In the rest of this chapter, we locate reflexive TA within the wider qualitative tradition and in relation to the theoretical underpinnings of knowledge production. We situate TA in relation to other modes of qualitative inquiry and emphasize some context for its use in the social sciences. The practicalities of the method are described in detail throughout the rest of the text using Braun and Clarke's (2006) six-phase approach. Before we get to the detail of how to do each phase of analysis, we delineate some often-overlooked elements that differentiate reflexive TA from other qualitative approaches.

## A FLEXIBLE ANALYTICAL METHOD

One of the key features of reflexive TA is its status as a method rather than a methodology (Braun & Clarke, 2006; Braun et al., 2018). *Methods* are the tools we use to do the tasks of research, slotted into wider research design, depending on the needs of our projects (Nicholls, 2009). When an approach comes fully loaded with (sometimes taken-for-granted) theoretical frameworks that shape a researcher's thinking about a research problem, and combinations of tools that support and enable a qualitative research project, they are *methodologies*. Although reflexive TA has a number of assumptions or values associated with it, these are to ensure its utility across a wide range of possible uses (including with different data collection methods and any number of theoretical perspectives). Because of this emphasis on flexibility, understanding the project's theoretical perspective before getting to the detail of the method is key to success.

All research needs to be located within a theoretical orientation; understanding and selecting from the different theoretical frameworks (and the philosophies that underpin them—see Table 1.1) can be complex but should not be avoided. Even when a theoretical framework is taken for granted or assumed within a discipline, understanding your theoretical position is still essential. This does not mean knowing everything, but having a working knowledge of your research framework and its relationship to other frameworks is a great starting point.

**TABLE 1.1. Theoretical Perspectives, Methodologies, and Reflexive TA**

| Theoretical perspective/paradigm | Positivism | Postpositivism | Interpretivism/constructivism | Radical/critical | Poststructural |
|---|---|---|---|---|---|
| Example methodologies | Scientific method | Mixed methods Qualitative Descriptive | Phenomenology Hermeneutics Grounded theory Ethnography IPA | Critical social theory Feminist theory Indigenous frameworks | Discourse analysis New materialist Posthuman |
| Appropriateness of TA as an analytic method | Not appropriate | Realist versions of TA (see Chapter 6) and potentially critical realist versions appropriate | Realist, critical realist, and relativist versions of TA appropriate | Critical realist and relativist versions of TA appropriate | Relativist versions of TA and thematic discourse analysis both appropriate (see Chapter 6) |

*Note.* IPA = interpretative phenomenological analysis; TA = thematic analysis.

Most people who have studied the social sciences (especially psychology) will be familiar with positivism, even if they have not heard it explicitly called that. Positivism is the key theoretical framework typically associated with scientific methods, and for many, quantification, hypothesis testing, and experimentation are indistinguishable from science overall. However, as you can see in Table 1.1, there is much more to knowledge production than the scientific method and certainly the type of thinking associated with positivism. It is worth considering that the philosophical underpinnings of each theoretical perspective inform the ways researchers look at the world, research, the nature of reality (ontology), theories of knowledge (epistemology), and the values of the researcher (axiology), even if they are not always explicitly acknowledged. Methodologies are often a product of these theoretical perspectives, allowing researchers a framework to think about their research question and the research process in a coherent fashion.

Historically, most qualitative research methodologies were developed (particularly within psychology) in opposition to positivism's dominance over knowledge production (Stainton Rogers & Willig, 2017). These developments highlighted different ways to engage with people and their perspectives on the world. Each move "away" from positivism comes with more complexity and a greater reliance on theory, philosophy, and interpretation to explore the phenomenon in question (and especially the "status" of people's talk and experiences). Certainly, there is no one right way to do research or produce knowledge, and your approach will depend on your research questions, your discipline, and the types of problems you are interested in addressing (Braun & Clarke, 2013; Grant & Giddings, 2002).

Some qualitative approaches are essentially a "methodological package," which provides inbuilt assumptions that can give researchers a clear direction on where to begin their journey to understanding. For instance, the analytical output of interpretative phenomenological analysis (IPA) is broadly thematic, working to describe patterns across (thematizing) and within (idiographic) interviews (Eatough & Smith, 2017). However, its theoretical foundations are inseparable from the procedures it uses (Smith et al., 2009). Indeed, IPA draws on multiple tools, including those needed for data collection (interviews, often repeated with the same participants), assumptions about samples (smaller participant numbers, homogeneity), and approaches to analysis (both idiographic and thematic—focusing analysis on individual participants and patterns across participants). These tools are explicitly wedded to its phenomenological theoretical focus that centers human experience and the particularities of individual lives and the interpretative lens needed by the researcher to help make sense of these

(Smith & Osborne, 2003). These inbuilt assumptions and packaging of tools are what you might expect from a methodology.

In contrast, when using reflexive TA, these decisions or expectations are not built into (or assumed within) the method. Instead, TA is simply a tool for qualitative data analysis. This does not mean that TA is atheoretical, rather that it was primarily designed to be theoretically flexible, usable as an analytic method across a variety of theoretical perspectives (Braun & Clarke, 2006; Terry et al., 2017). However, sometimes reflexive TA becomes aligned with particular frameworks. Historically, this has been phenomenological research, but more recently, people have assumed TA is "just a postpositivist method." These are certainly not the only theoretical frameworks within which TA can be used! The one caveat here would be positivist-informed research; the expectations and assumptions within positivism immediately clash with the core values of reflexive TA, especially its theoretical flexibility. Importantly, this flexibility means that researchers need to make well-informed choices and build reflexive TA into their research design—with TA akin to a single jigsaw piece in a puzzle. Without the other pieces surrounding it, its value is limited.

Reflexive TA's flexibility means it becomes important for the researcher(s) to identify their theoretical orientation because this will define the way TA is used. Unlike the wider, established theoretical perspectives referred to in Table 1.1, these possibilities tap into the core questions one would need to think about in terms of their theoretical framing. These positions should also be viewed as sitting on a continuum (Madill et al., 2018; Terry et al., 2017), rather than strictly polarized dichotomies. We flesh out these ideas with more detail and examples in Chapter 6.

The researcher could take up a position anywhere along this continuum, depending on the research topic in question and the focus of the researcher. For instance, researchers wanting to explore people's first-person descriptions of a phenomenon would find an *experiential* orientation most valuable. For others interested in the social structures that produce, enable, and constrain experience, a *critical* orientation might be relevant. While both could involve generating data from people's responses to questions of one kind or another, the analytical orientation would shape how these data were interpreted and reported.

Another question relates to the view of reality that the researcher applies to the data (their choice of ontology). For some, a *realist* position—where people's words are understood to provide direct access to participants' social, psychological, and physical reality—might drive the project (see Chapter 6 for an example). In other projects, a *relativist* position might be taken. Here, the ways participants' words draw on shared meaning-making tools (i.e., discourses) and help (re)produce particular realities within a given culture are important (see Chapter 6 for examples). Between these two perspectives, a *critical realist* analysis draws on elements of both—where an underlying reality might be recognized but seen as mediated through the multiple social realities of participants and the wider culture (Willig, 2013).

## WILL THE "REAL" TA PLEASE STAND UP?

The ubiquity of TA and its historically fuzzy boundaries with other analytic methods has sometimes meant people are a bit confused about what makes reflexive TA distinct from other thematizing methods. Obviously, there is no "real" or "true" version of TA, but there are differences between various versions of TA. A lack of recognition that there are different schools of TA (see Braun et al., 2018, for more detail) has resulted in a lot of method "blurring." In practice, this means that a report citing Braun and Clarke's (2006) paper as their method may give descriptions of processes that bear no relationship to the procedural elements Braun, Clarke, and their colleagues have described. We emphasize that understanding the approach that you are using, or referring to, is best research practice.

Reflexive TA has been designed to be a fully qualitative and interpretative way to do analysis—what has sometimes been called a *Big-Q* approach to qualitative research (Kidder & Fine, 1987). Big-Q research can be contrasted with *small-q* qualitative approaches, where the latter uses qualitative data, but in a way that is closely aligned with the traditional "scientific" methods of positivism (e.g., asking whether these data are reliable or whether they might be made numerical or tested statistically; Braun et al., 2018). In contrast, those who conduct Big-Q qualitative research are interested in resonance, transferability, and situating the research within a particular context. These researchers are not concerned with the truth, but rather producing knowledge which represents situated truths, where the researcher—informed by theory and an understanding of a research area and culture—can bring insight into that area. For researchers using the procedures of reflexive TA, the measure of rigor is not reliability but rather engagement with the data. This engagement is produced through the six phases of TA:

1. A thorough and ongoing *familiarization* with the data set (see Chapter 3).

2. An open-ended, organic *coding* process not constrained by concerns about agreement between different coders, nor by delimiting and defining codes (see Chapter 3).

3. *Initial theme generation* of tentative prototype themes from codes (see Chapter 4).

4. *Developing and reviewing* and testing those prototype themes against the data and developing them as needed, which will potentially involve a process of deconstruction and rebuilding new themes (see Chapter 4).

5. *Defining and naming* final themes (see Chapter 4), which serves as the basis for

6. *Writing up* the report (see Chapter 5).

Interpretation of data within reflexive TA comes from the interaction of the researcher's theoretical orientation and what they bring to the analysis while remaining answerable to the data set (i.e., your interpretations should remain grounded in the data). The reflexivity of reflexive TA, then, is concerned with reflecting on one's assumptions, treating yourself as the first object of study in a research project, not to limit or constrain the self, but to acknowledge what you bring to interpretation (your theoretical orientation and analytic choices). Big-Q qualitative researchers recognize that we are all situated in a context and see and speak from that position (see also Finlay & Gough, 2003).

Reflexive TA sits in relation to a broad family of theme-oriented analytic methods that include various "schools" of TA (Braun et al., 2018) and even different types of content analysis (CA; Hsieh & Shannon, 2005; see Figure 1.1). It is also worth noting that the analytical tools of methodological approaches such as grounded theory and IPA can also do similar thematizing work (Madill & Gough, 2008). Despite this variety, it is not uncommon for people to think of TA as a homogenous entity or (sometimes and) a generic approach to qualitative analysis (e.g., Boyatzis, 1998; Willig, 2013). We argue that it might be better to view the constellation of

**FIGURE 1.1. Continuum of Horizontal "Theming" Methods**

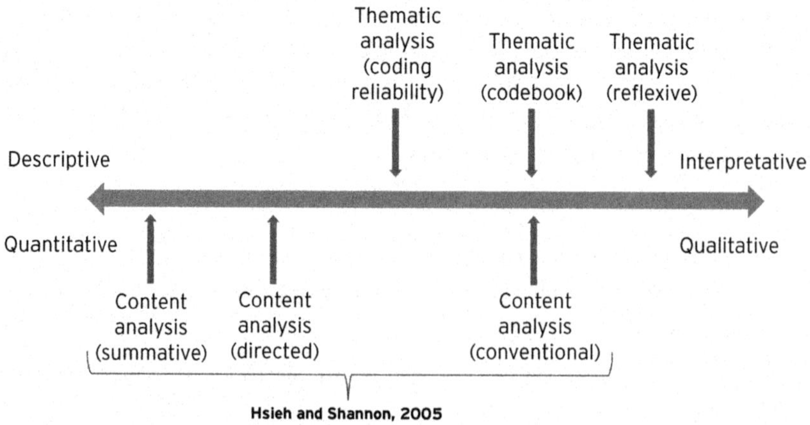

Hsieh and Shannon, 2005

*Note.* Derived from work by Nicola Kayes, with permission.

various qualitative theming methods as analogous to the hominid evolutionary tree. Although there may be a shared "ancestor" (probably an early version of "quantitative" content analysis; Braun et al., 2018; Merton, 1975), multiple offshoots have arisen that attempt to meet the specific needs of the environment (disciplinary, culturally, and even the worldviews) in which they develop. As a consequence of their shared ancestral history, there are often overlaps and continuities (e.g., beginning analysis with familiarization, using some form of coding), but the specific conditions each version arose in have produced different assumptions (e.g., familiarization produces a vastly different output in different methods—for some, it provides notes and initial thinking about the data; for others, patterns or even something close to themes are produced).

Braun and Clarke have identified three distinct schools of TA (see Braun et al., 2018). Although not all researchers using these different expressions of TA would refer to their method using the nomenclature of "schools," they would likely recognize the features that are described. Alongside (a) *reflexive* TA, there are (b) *coding reliability* versions of TA and (c) *codebook versions* of TA (see Chapter 6 for examples). Each school's approach to TA can be distinguished by different theoretical concerns (and even values), often tending to produce different kinds of output (themes, categories, domain summaries—see Chapter 4) and, most importantly, being defined by their answerability to either a quantitative or qualitative lens (see Figure 1.1).

In contrast to reflexive TA, coding reliability forms of TA can be considered only partially qualitative—because they are still primarily answerable to quantitative concerns (small-q research). For instance, Boyatzis (1998) indicated that his version of TA is a useful bridge for mixed methods research, enabling the findings of quantitative research to be blended with qualitative work—as long as quantitative "culture" (e.g., mainstream psychological research based on traditional scientific values) defines the terms of analysis. Because of this singular lens, coding reliability TA contains quantitative concerns about reliability, bias, replicability, and a single objective and discoverable truth, hence it is constrained to a realist ontology (that the world can be accessed through our senses in a straightforward manner). This contrasts with a Big-Q ideal that mixed methods researchers are bicultural (Kidder & Fine, 1987). Coding reliability TA generally uses a codebook, establishing a constrained number of codes agreed on by the researchers early in analysis, then uses consensus coding between two or more researchers to ensure analysis is as close to a version of the "truth" of analysis as possible (Joffe, 2012). They often use a statistic (Cohen's kappa) to determine the level of agreement between coders. Finally, there is an expectation that the researcher codes data to fit into predetermined groupings that tend to be closer to categories or domain summaries (see Chapter 4). Even with only a little knowledge about TA, it is likely becoming clear that coding reliability approaches are very different from the core values of reflexive TA.

Versions of codebook TA are more diverse than coding reliability approaches. It is quite common for codebook versions of TA to have been "rebranded," which can make them slightly harder to distinguish as forms of TA. Codebook versions of TA might also be known as template analysis (see King, 2012), framework analysis (see Ritchie & Spencer, 1994), or matrix analysis (see Miles & Huberman, 1994). Codebook versions of TA sit somewhere between coding reliability and reflexive versions of TA (see Figure 1.1). Codebook versions of TA are qualitative in orientation and philosophy but still seem to answer quantitative concerns (see the earlier discussion). This is particularly in the structuring of the coding process, often done in a specific way in the name of "rigor" (or even legitimacy—see Varpio et al., 2017). Themes are developed early in the process, in what we would think of as the familiarization phase of reflexive TA. A smaller proportion of data is initially analyzed to develop a set of codes (recorded in a codebook, often with definitions), which are then applied almost deductively to the rest of the data set. The outputs of codebook TA can be quite sophisticated, but the earlier development of themes predisposes confirmation rather than challenging or developing thematic constructs.

We introduce these different manifestations of TA, with similar names and processes, because they are often a source of confusion for people new to qualitative research. However, simply being aware that there are different types of TA is an important leap in understanding. Knowing your approach, what it offers, and what it constrains is central to doing any type of analysis well. When we outline the approach to reflexive TA in later chapters, note that elements such as developing a coding framework, testing for coder reliability, and member checking are considered incongruous with reflexive TA. These elements are not simply technical steps, minor differences, or easily aligned methods, they are (often) evidence of theoretical assumptions being built into various methods without questioning (Braun & Clarke, 2013, 2016; Smith & McGannon, 2018).

## CONSTRUCTED THEMES AS THE PRODUCT OF REFLEXIVE TA

The construct of "themes" has pervaded the common lexicon both within qualitative research and more widely in the general community. This is to the point that everyone knows, or thinks they know, what a theme is and what it does—this is both a problem and a resource. We view themes as meaning-based patterns constructed by researchers from raw data through a rigorous, systematic process to help tell the story of the data from a research project. However, it is common in some methods or approaches to TA to view themes as somehow preexisting in a data set. Within this common-sense framing, themes "emerge," or are "identified" by researchers and nonresearchers alike. They are "spotted" in the wild, as if data were a dark and mysterious forest in which rare mystical animals (themes) live, awaiting discovery. One simply arrives at the forest and begins searching to find these rare creatures—as if they were the Pokémon of qualitative data.

Emergence is assumed within this rubric: By looking long enough, pre-existing patterns will become self-evident and (perhaps more importantly) evident to those around you. It is the mysteriousness of the process that seems problematic to us, as if "finding themes" simply happens with ease and a straightforward process of uncovering what fundamentally already exists within the data set. All analysis involves hard work, and in our experience, a lot of thinking and reflecting (on ourselves and the data) and considerable chunks of time over long periods. Initial ideas were developed, data revisited, and meanings interpreted (and often reinterpreted) as we immersed ourselves within and made sense of the meanings of data sets. Nothing seemed ready and waiting to emerge!

A number of researchers (e.g., Braun & Clarke, 2019a; Humble & Radina, 2019; Sandelowski, 2007; Terry et al., 2017; Varpio et al., 2017) have argued that an emergence ideal can be problematic due to two related problems. First, it can subtly undermine the considerable effort (and researcher creativity) that goes into developing themes from a data set that does not have an inherent thematic structure. For instance, semistructured interviews tend to follow different directions, orientations, and flow, dependent on the skill of the interviewer, the perspectives of the participant, and the coconstruction of the interview itself (Braun & Clarke, 2013; Brinkmann, 2013; see also Chapter 2, this volume). Constructing patterns from this complexity involves a lot of work and close attendance to the data set. Second, because the expectation that "themes will emerge" is such a dominant idea, there is pressure on the researcher (particularly the novice researcher) to show that they can easily "spot" these themes. We have found that this can often result in the reduction to the lowest common denominator groupings of ideas—what is obvious in the data—because this offers the least risk. However, this approach often produces simplistic, superficial, single-note "themes" that are closer to summaries, categories, or other basic groupings of data (see Chapter 4). We completely understand the sense of vulnerability and anxiety involved in producing themes that go beyond the obvious, but that should not motivate limiting the interpretive possibilities of analysis. We see interpretation as a vital part of making sense of the data and producing a strong reflexive TA.

We strongly advocate for the position that qualitative data and analyses are cocreated by the researcher and their participants and not simply found (Braun & Clarke, 2006; Braun et al., 2018; Richards, 2014; Terry et al., 2017). We are also keen advocates of qualitative research and strongly believe that it is a skill that is learned and developed—similar to the skills learned in craft disciplines (e.g., blacksmithing, weaving). The processes we describe are simply avenues to reinforce the necessary skills and levels of engagement with data that are necessary to give a good account of the analysis of a data set. We hope that this text provides readers support and guidance regarding reflexive TA and also a shared language for researchers and their colleagues, supervisors and their students, editors and their reviewers, and authors.

# 2

## PROJECT DESIGN AND DATA GENERATION

In this chapter, the focus is on the design of your study—particularly, the research team, types of research questions, some of the methods that can be used to generate data for thematic analysis (TA), and how you might recruit your participants. We also introduce the illustrative projects we refer to through the remaining chapters to demonstrate the "doing" of reflexive TA. At this point, we reiterate that reflexive TA is just an analytic method. The discussion in this chapter is to provide pointers toward the types of design considerations a researcher using TA might work best with, rather than anything prescriptive. We aim to highlight the variation available in complementary methods, rather than giving the sense that reflexive TA is inherently a methodology in itself (see Chapter 1).

## RESEARCH TEAM CONSIDERATIONS

As with any research, the research team—including student–supervisor teams— needs to address various considerations when planning their project. These considerations include how ethics and data management will be managed, and by whom, to comply with the ethical and data protection requirements

https://doi.org/10.1037/0000238-002
*Essentials of Thematic Analysis*, by G. Terry and N. Hayfield

of the institutions and professional organizations (e.g., American Psychological Association, Australian Psychological Society, British Psychological Society, New Zealand Psychological Society) to which the researchers belong. There will also be pragmatic considerations about who will be responsible for what tasks (based partly on how much research experience each member has), how often you will meet, and how authorship will be decided. There is no specific size that a team should be; instead, the project is informed by pragmatic and contextual concerns, rather than any inbuilt expectations (e.g., whether the research is a student project, whether there are particular funding constraints).

Although working entirely alone is not common, independent working can, and is, done. However, most students will perform a TA with the support of their supervisors, and junior researchers with a senior member of staff. For large research projects, a team might typically consist of anywhere between three and six researchers, all reading the data and engaging in the phases of reflexive TA in a way that supports different perspectives being brought to the data analysis. Larger team sizes tend not to be common due to the pragmatics of organizing meetings and the collation of large quantities of analytic materials.

One key consideration in a TA study will be what different researchers bring to the project. Because reflexive TA centralizes the reflexive researcher, each researcher's contribution to design, recruitment, and data analysis needs acknowledgment and reflection. Researchers' differing perspectives on the data can be discussed among the team and incorporated during the analytic phases, but note that there is no requirement for all the researchers to reach unanimous agreement on all the data. Accordingly, particular frameworks for analysis advocated by some researchers, such as codebooks, inter-rater reliability, member checking, saturation, and confirmation bias, are not congruent with reflexive TA (see Chapter 1). Moreover, whereas other methods come with specific philosophical features built into the design, teams working on a TA will instead need to make a number of choices together about their approach to ontology, epistemology, and data analysis (see Braun & Clarke, 2016; Terry et al., 2017; Terry & Hayfield, 2020; see also Chapter 1, this volume). These are the specific types of considerations you might want to address working as a team on TA. We use the Person Centred Care study to illustrate some of these ideas.

***Introducing the Person Centred Care (PCC) Study.*** The Person Centred Care Study (Terry & Kayes, 2020) was a secondary analysis of interview and focus group data that had been collected for three projects in the Centre for Person Centred Research (PCR) at Auckland University of Technology. Researchers in the Centre had engaged in research over the course of a decade, exploring new ways of working for clinicians in the rehabilitation of patients following illness and injury. The researchers on this project sought to capitalize on the data sets generated to gain insight into how person-centered care was enacted in practice. Three projects were selected as representative of the Centre's wider data corpus and treated as a single data set, comprising 40 interviews with patients, family members, or carers; three focus groups with patients; two interviews with clinicians; and six focus groups with clinicians.

For this study, Gareth had begun work in PCR on its 10th anniversary. To help give some coherence to the story the Centre could tell about itself, given the soft-funded, project-by-project model it was built on, a secondary analysis of existing data sets was proposed. Although Gareth was the primary researcher for this project, others in the Centre had been involved in the original projects, and they acted in a consultative fashion. Rather than the team acting as a mechanism to confirm the analysis Gareth was performing, they provided useful contextualized information about the original data set, its participants, the reasons for various interpretations, and important theorization. In other words, the members of the team helped increase the quantity and variety of resources Gareth could use to construct the themes in the project. Nicola Kayes (one of the project leaders and the Centre's director) also participated in the analysis, particularly in theme development, where, again, her insight enhanced and added to Gareth's, rather than simply confirming the themes.

## RESEARCH QUESTIONS

The flexibility of TA (see Chapter 1) makes it suitable to address a broad range of research questions. The research question is central to any qualitative project and needs to be developed early to inform the design of your study. However, unlike quantitative studies, your research question is open to change. For example, you might start with a broad research question that, based on the data you collect, you later decide to narrow down, or perhaps expand out to a broader question than initially posed. Alternatively, you might find that your data are somewhat unexpected, which could necessitate a change of direction in your research question to capture the shift in focus. It is also possible that you will become interested in more than one aspect of the data set and therefore develop more than one research question—although the data need sufficient depth and diversity for this to work. Overall, it may be useful to think of your research question as a tool to guide the study design and the direction of your analysis, partly based on the data you collect and your early engagement with those data. Crucially, your research question must fit your epistemological and ontological approach and your method of data collection and be suited to your (TA) project (see Willig, 2013). Table 2.1 gives some examples of the types of research questions that psychologists have explored using TA, ranging from questions about people's lived experiences to how particular phenomena are perceived or represented through to how meaning is socially constructed.

## METHODS OF GENERATING DATA

The flexibility of TA is also apparent in the wide variety of data generation methods that can be suitable. The key is developing a strong rationale, ensuring that the data collection method best fits your topic, aims, and research question (see Willig, 2013). If you are interested in individual experiences and understandings of a topic, then interviews, diaries, surveys, or focus groups are examples of potentially appropriate forms of data collection. If you want to find out people's perspectives of a particular phenomenon—particularly if it is one in which they are not personally invested—focus groups, story completion tasks, or vignettes can all be a good fit. If you are keen to explore how aspects of a topic are constructed, the most suitable form of data collection will be dictated by how specific your interest is. For example, if you broadly want to identify how a particular topic is constructed, interviews, surveys, focus groups, or secondary sources would all be suitable. However, if your focus is on how your topic is constructed in the media, for example, you would need to decide what forms of media would be best for your analysis. There will also be pragmatic and ethical considerations that play a part in your decision. Table 2.1 shows some published studies and data collection methods researchers have selected to address their research questions and aims.

In this section, we briefly introduce some examples of methods of data generation that you could analyze using TA, although these are not exhaustive, and other forms of data collection can also be suitable (e.g., participant diaries, alternative forms of secondary data). Whichever data collection method you choose, remember to bear ethics in mind. The interaction between researcher and participant should be an ethical exchange, not simply extraction of information (Brinkmann & Kvale, 2017). There is nothing inherently ethical about qualitative research, so any high-quality data generation needs to be interwoven with a strong ethical philosophy, where informed consent, power, and risks of misuse of research skills are thought through and mitigated. At minimum you should ensure that information sheets clearly convey what the study involves

**TABLE 2.1. Examples of TA Studies, the Research Question, and Data Collection Type**

| Focus of research question | Research question | Data collection |
|---|---|---|
| People's experiences of particular aspects of their lives | How do business travelers experience time spent together and apart from their family—to examine how they attempt to balance work and family life (Nicholas & McDowall, 2012)? | Interviews |
| People's experiences of a particular phenomenon | What are users' experiences of online discussion forums about Parkinson's disease (Attard & Coulson, 2012)? | Online discussion forums |
| People's experiences and meaning making of particular aspects of their lives | What are the experiences and meanings associated with orgasm and sexual pleasure during sex with a partner (Opperman et al., 2014)? | Qualitative surveys (hard copy or email) |
| People's understandings, perspectives, or perceptions of particular aspects of their lives | What are lesbian, gay, and bisexual people's perspectives of how their sexual identity is relevant to their experiences of living with a chronic illness (Jowett & Peel, 2009)? | Qualitative surveys (online) |
| People's practices and/or how they make sense of particular practices | How do people make sense of and construct apparently counter-normative gendered body hair practices (Jennings et al., 2019)? | Story completion tasks |
| Influencing factors in relation to a particular phenomenon | What are the perspectives of participants with rheumatic disease on completing a daily diary about fatigue and well-being (Hegarty et al., 2019)? | Focus groups and interviews |
| Self-representations | How do heterosexual women represent themselves in online dating profiles (Wada et al., 2019)? | Online dating profiles |
| Representations of particular phenomena | How are men's extreme acts of violence against female partners represented within South African print media (Isaacs, 2016)? | Print media (newspaper articles) |
| Constructions and/or discourses of particular phenomena | How are difficult and rewarding aspects of cancer care for men and women constructed in relation to gender (Ussher et al., 2013)? | Semistructured interviews (telephone and face to face) |

*Note.* TA = thematic analysis.

(including through a clear title), that participation is voluntary, how confidentiality will be managed, how to withdraw, and sources of support so that potential participants are fully informed. If they decide to take part, they will need to provide their consent to do so.

## Face-to-Face Methods

### Interviews

Interviews are one of the earliest qualitative methods of data collection and remain the most popular and widely recognized. A key advantage of interviews is the opportunity to probe and ask follow-up questions, which can help to generate rich and detailed data. Interviews are most suited to when the participant is personally invested in the topic because this means that they are likely to have lots to say and can therefore provide you with the type of in-depth and detailed data that is ideal for TA (e.g., Braun & Clarke, 2013; Breakwell, 2012; Willig, 2013).

The most common types of interviews within qualitative research are in-depth and semistructured, where you create a schedule (or protocol) of open-ended questions to guide data collection. In Big-Q qualitative research (see Chapter 1), the researcher does not aim to necessarily ask the same questions of all the participants (Kidder & Fine, 1987). Interview questions need to be carefully designed but are also likely to be revisited and redrafted because early interviews can inform changes to the schedule for later ones. We recommend spending time creating the initial schedule and developing it during piloting and as data collection progresses. When designing your interview schedule, remember to have your research question at the forefront of your mind to help you stay on track. Initially, you might get started by jotting down questions based on your interest in the topic. Interview questions can also be inspired by reading what other researchers have asked participants, what topics seemed important in their analysis, and what suggestions they made for future research. Additional materials such as community-based and publicly available resources (often found on the internet) may also be useful in inspiring topics and questions.

Considerable guidance is available to help you think about the order and the types of questions to include in your interview schedule, as well as the sorts of phrasing you might use (e.g., Braun & Clarke, 2013; Breakwell, 2012; Flick, 2018; Silverman, 2013). Briefly, start with the broadest questions and become more specific as your schedule progresses (a design often referred to as an upside-down triangle), with broad open questions at the top and narrower, more specific questions at the bottom. When conducting research on sensitive or personal topics, begin with easy questions so that participants are eased into talking. They are then more likely to feel able to answer more difficult questions later on as they become comfortable with you and the research setting. How structured an interview schedule is will depend on your preferences (and those of your research team), but your schedule is a tool to guide the interview rather than something to which you strictly adhere.

We tend to organize our interview schedules by levels. First, we write headings that capture the topic areas we want to cover, then we develop broad questions, followed by potential probes based on the types of issues we anticipate might arise. However, it is important to be flexible and listen to what your participant is saying so that you can follow up on their talk and allow them to lead the interview. You are not aiming to ask the same questions of all your participants, nor in the same order. Sometimes a particularly keen participant might answer lots of your questions within the first few minutes— although you may also want to circle back to explore their answers more fully during the interview.

In qualitative interviews, the schedule acts as a guide for the interview, but the data that are generated are led partly by the researcher and partly by the participant and what they feel is important to discuss (sometimes interviews are referred to as *coconstructed*). In this sense, the interview can be understood as somewhat akin to a "conversation that has a structure and a purpose" (Brinkmann & Kvale, 2015, p. 5). There are also increasingly recognized and commonly used variations, including telephone and video (e.g., Skype) interviews, which tend to be conducted with minimal difference in data quality (see Hanna, 2012; Hanna & Mwale, 2017; Novick, 2008). You might like to consider providing your participant with a list of topics that you will ask about, in advance, making clear that you may not follow these in order so that they have an opportunity to think about them before the interview.

The researcher's task is to keep the conversation on track so that the data will be useful for your research (Brinkmann, 2013). We recommend practicing your questions and knowing your schedule so that during the interview, you notice what has been covered and avoid repeating yourself. Whether you are conducting interviews in person or via telephone or video, knowing your schedule can help ensure full engagement without looking at your questions—doing so can interrupt the flow and be distracting for both you and your participants. If their talk is not relevant to your topic, you can gently guide them back on topic—although sometimes it is hard to determine what might actually be important; this is a skill you can develop. Scholars have written papers, chapters, and even entire books on developing interview schedules and interview skills. Therefore, it would not be possible to include sufficient guidance for novices on interviewing within this short text, so we recommend looking at additional sources if you are unfamiliar with interview techniques (e.g., Braun & Clarke, 2013; Flick, 2018).

### Focus Groups

Focus groups, also referred to as group interviews, have some similarities to interviews. However, there are also differences. In focus groups, the researcher's role is that of moderator, and the aim is to encourage participants to generate a group discussion by talking to each other—rather than participants responding directly to the researcher—which can potentially make focus groups a way to capture a broad range of opinions. Designing a focus group guide is not unlike developing an interview schedule, although organizing and running focus groups may be somewhat different from planning and conducting interviews, and there are certainly increased opportunities for participants' talk going off topic (Braun & Clarke, 2013; Millward, 2012).

One additional consideration is who each focus group is made up of (e.g., homogenous or heterogenous groups; participants who are friends, acquaintances, or strangers; participants who are knowledgeable or naive about the topic; people who are invested or not in the topic; see Braun & Clarke, 2013; Willig, 2013). Another consideration is the skills you might require in managing individuals within the group. It is not uncommon, for example, for some people to dominate the discussion or to contribute little; reading up on these types of issues beforehand can help you prepare for such occurrences. Some researchers have argued that how participants interact with each other, and how this informs the generation of data, is an often-overlooked aspect of focus groups and one that deserves attention (e.g., Braun & Clarke, 2013; Millward, 2012). You can also be creative, using stimulus materials or group activities to instigate discussion. While less extensively used or written about compared with interviews, focus groups have gained in popularity. Various authors have written chapters in qualitative research textbooks which include extensive guidance on designing and running focus groups, including pragmatic issues such as organizing for multiple participants to be available at the same time, and ethical considerations about group discussions and managing confidentiality appropriately (e.g., Braun & Clarke, 2013; Flick, 2018; Millward, 2012; Willig, 2013).

### Transcribing Data

Ideally, if you are using face-to-face data collection methods, you will audio record and transcribe them. Converting text from audio is not a straightforward process of capturing words on paper, and you may want to read guidance and reflections on transcription before you start (e.g., Bird, 2005; Sandelowski, 1994). Transcription is crucial to your research project and, while time consuming, it is important that this task is completed thoroughly and to a high standard—errors can significantly change the meaning of your data. Good transcripts are central to high-quality analyses and can also inform evolution in data collection processes. There are various specific notation guides available that set out how you can capture varying levels of detail in your written text. Which you choose to use will depend partly on your ontological and epistemological approach to the data, where it may be more or less important to capture details such as participants' emphasis on particular words or lengths of pauses (see Braun & Clarke, 2013). For instance, researchers doing postpositivist research will often "tidy up" their transcripts because these components are of less interest to those within this theoretical orientation. This makes transcripts closer to the sorts of speech you find in a novel or movie (often referred to as "intelligent verbatim"). In practice, this will mean adding punctuation but not "guggles" (all the verbal nods, affirming noises, agreements, etc.; see Braun & Clarke, 2013), hence all the ums and ahs, laughter, sighs, and repetition will be removed, and the interviewer components will be downplayed. We prefer to use full orthographic or verbatim transcripts, which contain all the elements listed previously because they help reflect the messiness of language and the meaning-making processes people engage in as they speak. Transcription is also an excellent opportunity to listen to the data and familiarize yourself with the content—the first phase of TA (see Chapter 3).

## Textual Methods

In this section, we provide a brief introduction to three forms of textual data collection, which could all be suitable for TA studies. In textual methods of data collection, you do not meet your participant in person but instead ask them to provide written responses, for example, to survey questions, a story cue, or a vignette (see the following sections). Textual methods have been gaining in popularity over the last 10 years or so, although to date, relatively little has been written about them (Braun et al., 2017; Clarke et al., 2017; also see Clarke et al., 2019, for an introduction to a special issue of *Qualitative Research in Psychology* on story completion). Many textual methods have their roots in quantitative research but have been adapted by qualitative researchers due to their various advantages. These advantages include not needing to be present while participants complete their responses and not needing to transcribe data from audio recordings, making these methods much less time consuming and resource light than face-to-face methods. Further, participants have a sense of "felt anonymity," which can mean that textual data collection is particularly suited to exploring personal or sensitive topics. Textual methods are especially useful for qualitative researchers new to qualitative research because of the reduced ethical concerns brought about by not needing to meet participants face to face. However, in not meeting your participants, you will be unaware of their nonverbal and/or emotional responses to your questions. This potential ethical concern about not being able to gauge participant reactions to the task makes it especially important to carefully design your information sheet so that it fully informs participants about what to expect and provides appropriate support services—particularly if you are researching sensitive topics.

You will also need to consider other practicalities such as recruitment and in what format to collect your data. These methods offer opportunities to recruit hard-to-find populations (because participants can be recruited from a wider geographical reach than if you were traveling to meet them) and to some extent to reach those who are beyond the usual middle-class, White, well-educated samples (because they can be completed in a variety of modes and at a time and place convenient for a range of participants). Most commonly, textual data are collected online using software such as SurveyMonkey and Qualtrics, but you could distribute email or hardcopy versions. However, the latter will take some effort and require consideration of how effectively the mode of data collection might impact on reaching particular groups. Finally, while the data do not need transcription, you will need to factor in time to type up or transfer responses from data collection software ready for analysis.

## Surveys

Qualitative surveys typically consist of between four and 12 open-ended questions to which participants are asked to provide written responses. Surveys are particularly flexible and are suitable whether you aim to focus on participants' experiences, practices, or understandings of a particular topic. When designing your survey, you will need to provide written instructions that are concise and easy to follow, ensure a good structure, and develop clearly worded open-ended questions. Unlike during face-to-face data collection, you will not have any opportunities to clarify, rephrase questions, or probe participants to say more. Therefore, the aim is to design questions that are easy to understand and that encourage participants to answer fully. If the questions are carefully developed, there is a greater potential for the data you collect to be sufficiently rich for your TA. Therefore, we recommend piloting with a few participants to see how well the survey questions are working (Braun & Clarke, 2013; Terry & Braun, 2017). To illustrate the value of TA in qualitative survey studies, we use the Body Hair and its Removal and Alteration (BHRA) survey in this text.

*Introducing the BHRA Survey.* Hair removal for women has been normative in most "Western" countries for some time, but body hair practices appear to have changed rapidly, with (younger) women removing more hair and many younger men also engaging in hair removal. In 2012, Virginia Braun and Gareth were interested in understanding how younger people (between 18 and 35 years of age) in Aotearoa/New Zealand feel about body hair and its removal and what they do with their own body hair. We developed a survey to address these questions. Over a short space of time, we gathered 584 completed surveys from female (50.6%), male (48.9%), and "other" identified (0.5%) people. In this book, we use data collected from the gay and bisexual men in the sample about the hair removal practices. These data have been analyzed and published as part of the wider male sample (see Terry & Braun, 2016) but have not been reported separately.

## Story-Based Methods: Story Completion Tasks and Vignettes

Story completion tasks are a novel form of data collection that are becoming increasingly popular within psychology and other disciplines (Braun et al., 2017; Clarke et al., 2017, 2019). Participants are presented with a story stem or cue and asked to write a story about what happens next. Vignettes, which are to some extent a cross between story completion and surveys, often use some form of moral dilemma for participants to respond to. Participants are presented with a scenario—or a series of scenarios—with questions about the scenario(s). There is lots of flexibility in the types of questions you ask at each stage of a vignette. They might be open-ended questions about the scenario or about the characters and what they "could" or "should" do—expect the wording you choose to potentially make a difference to the responses you receive. Alternatively, or in addition, participants could be asked to write a story about what happens next—as in story completion. In story-based methods there is no requirement for participants to take ownership of what happens to the characters in their story (with the exception of some vignette studies that ask participants what they would do in response to the given scenario). The focus on the hypothetical makes story-based methods a good choice for topics that could otherwise produce socially desirable responses (e.g., climate change, drug use, sexual behaviors).

Story completion and vignettes require careful and considered designs. The scenarios need to be engaging and provide sufficient detail to set the scene without giving too much information, which might result in participants' responses being constrained by the design. Story completion and vignette data can be unpredictable, so piloting is vital to ensure that participants understand the instructions to increase the potential for rich data to be produced. We suggest you look at examples and read about the various elements of design before going ahead with your study (Braun & Clarke, 2013; Clarke et al., 2017; Gray et al., 2017). The following gives some details of the menopause study we use in the following chapter.

***Introducing the Menopause and Perimenopause Story Completion Study.*** Nikki Hayfield and colleague Christine Campbell developed this project to explore undergraduate students' perceptions of menopause and perimenopause. Participants were 102 psychology students (93 women, nine men) who were offered a course credit for participation. Students were shown a brief stem describing a character called Kate, who notices that her periods are changing. Kate mentions this to a friend, who suggests to Kate that she might be starting to go through menopause. Participants were then invited to write a story of at least 200 words about "what happens next" in Kate's life over the following days, weeks, months, or years. They were advised that they could introduce other characters and describe how Kate is feeling and what experiences she has. Hannah Moore was a research assistant who worked on the early phases of the project.

## DETERMINING SAMPLE SIZES

You will need sufficient numbers of participants and quality of data to produce patterns across your data set that can then be developed into themes through your engagement with the data. Because themes are generated rather than "excavated" or "emergent" in reflexive TA (see Chapters 1 and 5), mechanisms to determine sample sizes through "information redundancy" (Lincoln & Guba, 1985), or saturation, are not particularly relevant (see Braun & Clarke, 2019b). Instead, decisions about participants and participant numbers are largely pragmatic ones, based on factors such as how many participants who meet your inclusion criteria you can recruit within your timescale and whether the data you have generated look rich enough to identify meaningful patterns.

The type of data collection you use is an important factor in determining sample size (for discussions of the methods referred to earlier, see, for example, Braun & Clarke, 2013; Breakwell, 2012; Flick, 2018; Gray et al., 2017; Terry & Braun, 2017; Terry et al., 2017). Your sample need not necessarily be homogenous, although it can be more likely that you will be able to construct patterns of meaning in smaller samples if there are similarities in the demographics of your participants. If your participants are demographically diverse, you may require more people to take part to have sufficient data to construct shared and meaningful patterns across them.

The following figures are general guidance for the smallest advisable numbers for a TA project. If you intend to publish your research, we recommend looking at published examples within different journals because requirements may vary. If conducting interviews, each participant will likely make a considerable contribution (data items are "thicker"), so six to 10 participants might be sufficient. The number of participants in your focus groups plays a part in the quality of the data and therefore how many are needed, but two to four groups would be a minimum. If you conduct surveys, each participant will contribute data that are less rich than in interviews or focus groups (data are "thinner") due to the lack of opportunity for the researcher to encourage in-depth responses. Therefore, no fewer than 15 to 30 participants will likely be required—but the quality of responses plays a part in deciding the number of participants.

For story completion tasks and vignettes, it is difficult to recommend numbers because these methods are novel, and the depth of participants' responses vary. If you have only one version of your story completion task or vignette, and participants fully engage, 15 responses might be enough. However, if you have more than one version of your story completion task or vignette or recruit from groups who are less invested in your research, then 30 to 40 stories (or even more) might be needed as a minimum to enable you to construct patterns from the data. Secondary sources such as forums, newspaper articles, online blogs, and so on will vary enormously in quantity and quality, which will inform how many are needed.

In this chapter, we provided guidance on designing a research project and generating data. We introduced some particularly pertinent face-to-face and textual methods, all of which are suitable for TA studies. Once you have designed your study, recruited participants, and prepared your data, you can begin the analytic process, which we turn to in the following chapters.

# 3 DATA ANALYSIS

*Familiarization and Coding*

Reflexive thematic analysis (TA) consists of six phases: (a) familiarization, (b) coding, (c) initial theme generation, (d) developing and reviewing themes, (e) defining and naming themes, and (f) writing the report. These are referred to as phases rather than stages because you are not aiming to work through these in a linear way. A word of caution and some caveats, though. While we encourage you to use these phases recursively, it is poor practice to jump to themes before a rigorous familiarization (Phase 1) and coding (Phase 2) process because you will have only superficially engaged with the data (remember that TA is about ever-increasing and rigorous engagement with the data; see Chapter 1). Therefore, it is critical that you begin with the first two phases—becoming thoroughly familiar with the data and coding the entire data set—because these phases form the foundations of your analysis. In sum, we suggest that some phases will necessarily come before others, but nonetheless, we encourage you to try to avoid thinking of them as the step-by-step guidance of a "recipe" that you follow to produce your analysis and, instead, suggest using the phases iteratively and recursively to guide deep engagement with your data (Braun & Clarke, 2006; Clarke et al., 2015; Terry et al., 2017).

https://doi.org/10.1037/0000238-003
*Essentials of Thematic Analysis*, by G. Terry and N. Hayfield

For example, when you have coded the data (Phase 2) and generated some initial themes (Phase 3), you may find that during the developing and reviewing phase (Phase 4), you revisit coding (Phase 2), perhaps after a meeting of the research team where new ideas came to light. Or when producing the report (Phase 6), you may continue to develop your analysis in such a way that the themes and their names need to be revisited (Phase 5). Further, there are often multiple versions of writing reports (Phase 6). You might present at a conference and find that disseminating your results serves as a test of your analysis that helps you think slightly differently, which then informs further development of themes in a written report. It is particularly common to respond to feedback from supervisors and/or reviewers, which could inform you revisiting any, or all, of the phases. It is also worth noting that you write reports of the data analysis differently according to your audience (see Chapter 5 on writing up your analysis). For example, a summary of findings for participants needs to be written in accessible lay language, whereas a journal article will need to be more formal in style and meet the requirements of your discipline and chosen journal.

In this chapter, we discuss familiarization and coding. In the next chapter, we discuss theme development, which is made up of Phases 3 to 5. We mention the sixth phase when we discuss writing the manuscript (Chapter 5), which in TA is part of the analytic process because writing involves interpretation, structuring, and decisions about data extracts. We include examples based on our data from three research studies to demonstrate the phases of TA (see Chapter 2 for an introduction to these studies).

## PHASE 1: FAMILIARIZATION

To produce a strong TA, you will first need to become familiar with all your data. Familiarization is an active engagement with the data as data, reading with the purpose of immersing yourself in your data set. This may seem a daunting task, particularly if you have a large data corpus. However, as high-lighted earlier, it is important to engage fully with familiarization and coding because these early phases provide the underpinnings of a strong TA. Aspects of your data collection and generation might form part of this familiarization process in that you start to become familiar with your data as you conduct and transcribe interviews and focus groups or as you read responses to surveys, story completion tasks, and vignette studies.

In face-to-face methods of data collection, you will be attentive during the interview or focus group, and you will likely contemplate what was said afterward—you might want to keep a research journal to help you reflect on the process of data collection and document your initial noticings (see also Braun & Clarke, 2013). Your early familiarization may even further inform your data generation. For example, you might slightly change your semi-structured interview schedule, or your textual data collection materials, as a consequence of musings on early data collection—and we note that this is common practice (Brinkmann, 2013; also see Chapter 2, this volume). You can also think about transcription as a key opportunity to become familiar with your material—transcription is not simply a technical step in data collection. Of course, it may be that you are not the primary transcriber of your data or that you are not directly involved in the data collection phase. If this is the case, you could listen to audio recordings and ensure that you read through the written responses to "catch up" on this first phase of familiarization. Even if you have collected the data yourself, reading the data set in its entirety at least once is also a crucial part of familiarization. In sum, whenever you read or listen to data, even early on in your research, try to approach this as an aspect of data familiarization. You might like to think of analytic engagement as akin to analyzing a text for an English literature course—which would be in contrast to how you might read a lighthearted novel. In familiarization, you engage with the data by immersing yourself fully and thinking analytically.

We also recommend making familiarization notes about your initial observations of the data. These can be free flowing and capture your thoughts as you read and think about the content. If you are working with face-to-face data, you might want to make familiarization notes for each interview participant or focus group (see Exhibit 3.1) and perhaps an additional set of notes for the entire data set (see Exhibit 3.2). Finding ways of splitting the data up can make familiarization feel manageable. For example, you could make notes on sections of data organized by different groupings (e.g., participant gender, responses to a particular question within a survey, different versions of a vignette or story completion, or starts, middles, and endings of story completion data—also see Exhibit 3.3). These notes are purely to help you become familiar with your data set. You do not have to share them—although you could (e.g., with the research team or in the appendices of a dissertation or thesis to document your analysis).

Try to be relaxed and avoid becoming anxious about familiarization. This phase is the starting point of your analysis, and the purpose is to get to know the data before you engage with them more systematically during coding. Sometimes we are asked whether the researcher really needs to become familiar with the entire data set before coding, and the answer is an unequivocal "yes." The more you do during this early part of the analytic process, the less likely it will be that you will miss key ideas, and you will be in a stronger position when you code and analyze the data.

The following are some tips for familiarization:

- Put yourself in an analytic mindset from early on—you might want to think critically and take an investigative approach, perhaps interrogating your data by asking questions such as who, what, when, where, why, how, and what does this mean—although, at this point, you are still taking a casual rather than a systematic approach.

- Consider data collection as part of the familiarization process.

- Keep a research journal to help you reflect on what you are bringing to data generation and how this helps you notice ideas in the data, or consider what you might be missing (perhaps through discussing the data with others). This should happen as you are generating and working with your data and provides a space for you to engage in reflexivity, which can assist in the formation of early analytic insights.

- When you listen to audio recordings or read written responses, try to fully engage, hearing or reading your data as data (see earlier) and immersing yourself in them.

- Be curious about your data, and repeatedly ask questions of them (see above), to help you think about them in different ways or from different perspectives.

- Make familiarization notes in a separate notebook about what you find interesting, intriguing, or even puzzling about the data. These notes are primarily about your observations of the data and are therefore different from your research journal, but the contents could also arise from or build on some of your reflections.

At the end of this phase, you are aiming to feel as though you have become fully acquainted with your data and are ready to move to coding. In the following exhibits, we give some examples of familiarization notes from (a) an interview/focus group study (the Person Centred Care [PCC] Study; Exhibits 3.1 and 3.2) and (b) a story completion project where participants were asked to write a fictional account in response to a scenario about a hypothetical character going through perimenopause or menopause (with familiarization notes by Nikki's research assistant, Hannah; Exhibit 3.3). What will be evident from these examples is that familiarization is not a cut-and-dried process. Use whatever works for you, especially given different types of data. In Exhibit 3.1, you can see a small extract of the individual participant notes

**EXHIBIT 3.1. Familiarization Notes From an Interview Transcript From the Person Centred Care Study**

- Living with spasticity issues, removal of parts of leg, result of traumatic brain injury.
- Has built up a lot of knowledge over years. Likes to be treated as though he has something to contribute.
- Both parties learn from each other (especially with reference to student physios).
- Feeling like your rehabilitation is important, not just another person using up a therapist's time.
- The person doing the rehab needs to be able to wax and wane in motivation, and the therapist should be responding to that—client's schedule not the therapist's.
- Felt at times that his window to recover was limited by lack of therapist investment/ availability, compounded by physio talking about the recovery window being limited to 2 years.

that Gareth used for one of the subprojects of the PCC Study (his full notes per participant might typically be one to three typed pages).

At the end of data familiarization, it can be a good idea to develop notes for the whole data set. An extract of Gareth's wider notes for the PCC Study is in Exhibit 3.2. Note that although these contain big, compelling ideas, they are not in any way themes at this point. They might contain the seed of something, but it is worth avoiding talk about "what's coming out from the data" at this point. These are just noticings that will help shape and sharpen your coding processes. Familiarization also enhances the creative juices of the whole analytical process, and engagement and depth of knowledge act as a resource for the analyst.

Familiarization is also an opportunity for you to reflect on any emotional and early analytical responses to the data. This is not because you would be aiming to be "unbiased" or avoiding imposing ideas on the data you are reading, but rather to provide as many ways of thinking about the data set as

**EXHIBIT 3.2. Familiarization Notes for Entire Data Set From the Person Centred Care Study**

- There seems to be an ability to "transfer" trust between clinicians (positively and negatively).
- Lots of negative cases of care used—often to help highlight qualities of good care.
- Not just about independence for people?
- Clinicians acting as an "exoskeleton" or support mechanism?
- "Person centredness" seems often to be reduced to choice—informing patients as quickly as possible.
- Family/whānau included in decisions—is this always useful?
- Emphasis on physiological recovery. What about psychological implications?
- Clinician-centered practice or system's expectations?

possible. Within Big-Q approaches to analysis, and those that depart from positivist expectations (see Chapter 1), these sorts of reflections and responses are resources rather than inherently problematic. These reflections will help you acknowledge what your reading of the data looks like while remaining reflexive about how these ideas were generated. You could also discuss with supervisors, mentors, or a "critical friend" (someone who is willing to help you talk through your interpretations) using these notes to help frame the discussion.

You might choose to engage with data from surveys or story completion or vignette studies quite differently from interview or focus group studies, and there is no "correct way" to become familiar with your data. In Exhibit 3.3, Hannah engaged in familiarization in two stages. First, she made notes on how the stories began and ended, then she made further notes about the whole data set and ideas evident within the stories. This flexibility in approach can occur whether you work alone or as part of a team. The team might want to become familiar with the data and then meet to discuss your initial ideas, or you may prefer to work together as you familiarize yourself with the data. These are examples of strategies you might use to help provide insights into the data and should not be followed slavishly. They are simply a way of familiarizing yourself with your data set.

### EXHIBIT 3.3. Familiarization Notes From Perimenopause/Menopause Story Completion Data

Extract from Hannah's familiarization notes for story beginnings and endings:

P3: Starts with physical symptoms and difficulty with daily tasks/Ends with family and relationship difficulties due to symptoms and lack of understanding from others

P8: Starts with seeking medical assistance/Ends with adapting to menopause and having a normal life after the menopause

P32: Starts with panic when considering going through menopause/Ends with relationships being affected because of decreasing fertility through the menopause

P35: Starts with turning to the internet for information and consideration of identity being affected/Ends with acceptance of the menopause being a natural phase of life

P64: Starts with changes in periods characteristic of menopause/Ends with feelings of aging and feeling less attractive

P90: Starts with pregnancy worry/Ends with killing the man she is sleeping with

Extract from familiarization notes for ideas in the data set:

- The menopause is initially understood as a crisis—and this was commonly related to lack of fertility and being unable to have children and/or to fear of getting older.
- The age of the character was deliberately not stated. If participants mentioned age, then the character was either in their 20s and described as going through early menopause or was considered to be between 45 and 60 years old.
- The character sought information about the menopause on the internet, through their mothers and/or friends, and from a doctor (and often in that order).

## PHASE 2: CODING

Once you are familiar with your data and have a good sense of the content, you can move on to coding. In this phase, you will start to work with the data much more systematically and rigorously than during familiarization. This is not something that you can rush or do quickly—one of the key features of any qualitative analysis is the time it takes to fully engage in a suitably thorough and rigorous analysis of the data. The point of coding is to take your engagement with the data another level deeper and break them down into manageable chunks.

Before we leap into practicalities, it is necessary to outline what a code is. You could think of a *code* as a name or label that you assign to a chunk of the data. Coding serves two key purposes: (a) engaging with your data by interpreting and adding meaning to chunks of text and (b) reducing the volume of text to a list of codes. You might take an *inductive approach* to coding (bottom up), where the codes and themes are data driven, or a *deductive approach* (top down), where theory drives the coding and theming processes, or a mixture of both. This decision might be shaped by the overall approach to the use of TA (e.g., a researcher doing a relativist TA, informed by post-structuralist theory, might be more inclined to do deductive analyses than a researcher doing a realist TA, who will be more likely to take an inductive approach). These positions are hardly ever "pure" but sit on a continuum and are informed by your theoretical position (see Chapter 1). Whichever approach you take, we highly recommend thoroughly coding because, in the next phase, you will primarily work with your list of codes, rather than your raw data, when constructing your themes. Therefore, you are aiming for each code name to succinctly capture the meaningful content that is of interest to you.

One of the challenges in coding your data is assigning names or labels that capture the relevance of the data extract but that are brief enough to work with manageably. This can be difficult but is important. We recommend that the code label should convey a key point about the data without you having to see the original text to know what that point is. Therefore, we suggest aiming for codes to be a "short phrase" or "pithy label" that captures what is important in that bit of data (Braun & Clarke, 2013; Clarke et al., 2015, p. 235), without ending up with almost as many words from your codes as exist in your data, which would present challenges later on. When you begin coding, you will initially be creating lots of new codes, but as you progress, you will repeatedly assign existing codes to different extracts of data. Try to use existing codes where possible, without becoming complacent about new aspects of the data that are of interest and require a new code, or assuming that an existing code is "good enough." Equally, you might gain a new understanding of a particular topic as you code across the transcripts. This might mean that an existing code can be "improved"—it is worth going back to previous instances of the original code and seeing whether the improvement works there too. Exhibit 3.4 contains some codes generated from a short extract of the menopause stories.

We have noticed that novice researchers sometimes assign codes that are broad and often reliant on a single word for their code name. However, codes should not be too broad because you are aiming to capture something specific about the data. For example, in a project on students' perspectives on drinking at university, a researcher might assign a code of "socializing" to various chunks of data. However, were they to collate all instances of data coded as "socializing" into one document, they could find that the content was wide ranging, resulting in the meaning being lost. In this example, coded data might include instances of participants talking about how drinking is a part of socializing during first-year orientation (freshers or frosh) week at the start of their university course, discussing how drinking can be helpful to reduce inhibitions and to get to know people when socializing, or talking about how drinking seemingly goes hand in hand with socializing at university. In this case, we argue that the data needed to be broken down more. It could be that multiple codes (e.g., drinking as a first-year initiation, as an icebreaker, to lower inhibitions, as a social activity, as an inherent part of

---

**EXHIBIT 3.4. An Extract of Coded Data From the Menopause Study**

This exhibit shows a coded data extract with the codes assigned to each chunk of text in parentheses after the part they relate to. Note that some chunks of text are assigned more than one code (indicated by a backslash) and that elsewhere the same codes are assigned to different chunks of data.

Kate decides to seek advice from a doctor {*doctors as menopause experts*} as she is growing worried {*menopause cause for concern*}, and her friend agrees that this is the best course of action, even though Kate feels very embarrassed to do so {*doctors as menopause experts/visiting doctors* = embarrassing}. While she waits for her appointment, she decides to look into menopause herself {*lacks menopause knowledge/researching the menopause*}, as well as ask her mother what it will be like {*mothers as knowledgeable about menopause/menopause previously unspoken*}, which Kate remembers being very uncomfortable for her mother {*recalls and aware of mother's menopause/menopause as uncomfortable*}. She is concerned, as she is still quite young, that if she is about to go through menopause, she will be unable to have children {*menopause cause for concern/menopause seemingly at a young age/uncertainty of whether menopausal/menopause* = child crisis}, which would be devastating for her {*wants children/menopause ends possibility of (biological) child/to not have children would be devastating*}.

university social lives; never drinking alone) would capture more nuances in the data than wide-ranging codes would. This would then allow a fuller picture of how drinking and socializing can be understood in relation to the research question.

Indeed, when teaching TA, we have noticed that students overlook aspects of the data that we think are too important to be missed. One reason this might occur could be because it may seem that the content is too obvious to code. However, try not to take for granted that what is obvious to you is obvious to someone else. Overlooking important aspects of the data can also reflect a lack of full immersion in qualitative data to a sufficient depth. Therefore, particularly if you are new to data collection, we encourage you to engage in fine-grained coding, working with small chunks, and coding all that could potentially be relevant. It might be useful to think of coding as wringing out a wet cloth, where the aim is to squeeze as many codes out of your data as possible. It is important that you code all the data to help you fully engage with them. We also encourage researchers to make sure that they have breaks (which might include coffee, tea, and sweet treats) because this phase can be intensive and requires concentration and consistent engagement to ensure you are fully immersed in the data. For those who are more experienced in qualitative research, this level of fine-grained coding may not be as necessary. As researchers develop the analytic skills that come with practice, they tend to become more attuned to being immersed, without the need to code quite as closely. Nonetheless, we still advocate for ensuring that you code all the data that seem to be of possible relevance to your research question. Indeed, before you start coding, we recommend that you revisit your research question—perhaps even write it on a sticky note in front of you—so that you stay focused on thinking about which parts of the data relate to it and in what ways.

We have also noticed that many novice researchers tend to want to "jump ahead" to thinking about themes before they have coded all the data. While we advocate for a recursive approach, at this point, we encourage staying focused on codes to ensure thorough and methodical engagement with the entire data set before moving to themes. To keep this focus, you might want to jot down any ideas you are having for themes or relationships between codes so that you can get them out of your head and onto paper and then return to coding. If you start being prematurely distracted by what your themes might be, there is a risk of superficial engagement or partially coding the data corpus. The risk is that you will therefore not continue to engage as rigorously and might miss interesting aspects of the data. One example of this could be a particular participant's responses dominating your thinking and shaping your coding of the remainder of the data set. Therefore, you may want to move between transcripts to help try to avoid this. You might even need to do more than one round of coding, both to avoid particular participant responses shaping your data and because, as you progress, you might have new analytic insights, which means that revisiting earlier data becomes necessary to review them for ideas that developed later.

In reflexive TA, there are broadly two levels of coding: semantic and latent. *Semantic codes* stay at the surface level of the data and often capture or summarize a point that has been made by the participant. They stay close to participant meanings but are generally not their exact words. For example, in Exhibit 3.4, the extract "she is growing worried" is assigned the code "menopause cause for concern," which simply captures the meaning at the surface of the text. *Latent codes* tend to require more in-depth engagement with the data and capture something that lies beneath the data and requires interpretation on your part. They often draw on theory that you have gained in a substantive area of research. In contrast to deductive analyses, the labels for latent codes are informed by theory to help organize, rather than direct, what is looked for in the analysis. In the tips that follow, the code "continuum of care" is a latent code. It refers to something beneath the surface commentary that your existing knowledge helps you to identify. If you are new to qualitative analysis, it is likely that your initial coding will be somewhat more semantic than the coding of those with more experience. In contrast, as you become skilled at qualitative analysis and immersed in your data and subject area, it is more likely that at least some of your codes will be at a latent level.

Semantic codes fit well with experiential and realist approaches, whereas if you are working within more critical and relativist frameworks (see Chapter 1), latent codes are more likely to feature or even dominate. The chances are that you will have a mixture of semantic and latent codes, and at times, the distinction between the two may be somewhat blurry. It is important to remember that latent codes are not inherently "better" than semantic codes or vice versa. You will code according to (a) the needs of your project, (b) the level of immersion in the theory of a topic you are researching, (c) your approach to the data, and (d) your experience doing TA. It is also worth noting that codes may not tidily fit semantic or latent definitions, and in fact, in some ways, it does not matter which "type" of coding you use— what is more important is you making meaning from the data that adds to the depth of engagement you have in relation to them.

The following are some tips for coding data:

- You might like to think of this phase as a way to get to know your data intimately and to engage thoroughly with all the text more rigorously and at a much deeper level than during familiarization.

- You can also think of this phase as breaking the data into smaller chunks or meaningful pieces to help you manage the data and your analysis of them.

- The aim is to develop code names that are short but meaningful so that they tell you something specific about the content without you needing to see the data.

- Try to code carefully and systematically to ensure that you do not overlook data that could be relevant to your research question(s).

- Try to engage with the entire data set equally across all items—have plenty of breaks to help you stay fully engaged and consistently attentive to the data.

- Try to stay focused on coding and avoid jumping ahead to themes.

- Try to ensure that no single participant response comes to shape your entire coding process—you might want to move between accounts or revisit participant responses more than once and in a different order.

- Consider a second round of coding to ensure that all your ideas (including those that developed later in the coding process) are consistently captured across the data set.

- If you are coding as a team, you are not looking to produce identical codes or the "right" codes or create agreement between researchers. Instead, after initially coding independently, you can come together and discuss your codes. These codes can then all be considered to increase the diversity and number of resources you will need to construct themes. In other words, the benefits of working as a team are that you end up with more, rather than fewer, resources with which to work.

The format in which you code your data is also up to you. One option is to print off your data and code on a hard copy. In this case, we advise that you double space and leave wide margins and sufficient space to note codes. If you prefer working on a screen, you may want to use one of the many forms of computer-assisted qualitative data analysis software (CAQDAS). We have dabbled with these and, like others, have identified both advantages and disadvantages of them. We emphasize two points. First, it would be a mistake to think that using CAQDAS will do your analysis for you because in whatever form you organize and code your data, the primary analytic tool is you, the researcher (see also Braun & Clarke, 2013). Second, it can be easy to delete codes accidentally when trying to reorganize your framework, so it is advisable to back up data frequently. We recommend that if you are thinking about using software in your analysis, that you discuss it with others and read about it before trying it out.

In Exhibit 3.5, we provide another example of coding from the PCC Study. If you look back to Exhibit 3.4, you will see that these show two different styles of coding. We emphasize here that there is no right way to think about coding data, as long as it facilitates engagement.

Sometimes, we are asked how many codes should be generated during this phase. There is no easy answer because it depends on how large your data set is, how focused your research question is, how experienced you are as a researcher, how fine grained your coding is, and how you engage with the data more broadly. These statements apply whether you are working alone or as part of a team. Certainly, as a team, rather than reducing your codes down to produce a limited number of "agreed-on" codes, you can instead pool them and view them as a shared resource bank that you can build themes from together. If you have worked independently to come up with codes, meeting to discuss them and talk about similarities and differences can be useful but only insofar as it adds to team members' levels of engagement with the data. We suggest that meeting at the end of familiarization and coding phases should be the minimum requirements for doing a team-based TA (and a great idea for supervisor–student relationships too).

During coding, it may feel as though you are working at a microlevel of analysis, getting to know the data really well and noticing the finer details as

**EXHIBIT 3.5. Data Extracts and Codes From the Person Centred Care Study**

| Data extract | Code |
| --- | --- |
| Yeah, and also, I don't know if it's the usual practice, but my physio at [outpatient facility] actually took me out one day to [community clinic] and we met them, and I actually saw my physio and the physios there talking to each other and getting really excited and like talking about all these new plans for me and stuff, and it was sort of like just really important to see that handing over. And that was several weeks before I actually stopped at [outpatient facility], but still I knew that the seeds had been sown and [that] sort of thing and that I wasn't just going into a place that completely didn't understand me, and I had to build my whole sort of, yeah. [L2: So it was important you were part of that hand over?] Yeah, very. And that I had effectively actually been to the clinic before I, and we went there not intending to necessarily send me there. | • Physio going above and beyond<br>• Continuum of care<br>• Continuum of trust<br>• Transition managed through relationships<br>• Physios' excitement enabled engagement<br>• Importance of being understood<br>• Familiarity of new clinic important |

*Note.* Data from Terry and Kayes (2020).

you get deep into the text. This is important, but we endorse trying to notice what is happening at a more macrolevel too. The former is more likely to result in semantic codes, whereas the latter is conducive to producing latent codes. We argue that both "zooming in" to and "zooming out" from the data are requirements of coding to ensure that you complete the process thoroughly and rigorously. During the coding phase, you will have been working closely with your data, which means you are building on and enhancing your familiarity and engagement with the data. As you start developing themes (see Chapter 4), you can start to stand back and consider the codes you have generated and what might be happening across the data set, seeing them as the resources you will use to construct themes that tell the best story of your data set.

In this chapter, we explored the first two phases of reflexive TA, where the processes enable initial engagement with your data to more methodical structured engagement. We discussed the choices relating to coding and highlighted how codes can be understood as part of a resource to assist in constructing your themes. We move now to the next phases of theme construction and development.

# 4

# DATA ANALYSIS

*Theme Construction and Development*

By now, you will have a strong sense of the data set, pages of familiarization notes, and a long list of codes and their associated data. These are the resources or raw materials you need to build your themes to answer your research question—particularly your codes at this point. The move from codes to themes does not happen by magic but through your ongoing engagement with the resources you have created and your raw data—although there can be lightbulb moments of insight into the data.

## PHASE 3: INITIAL THEME GENERATION

Theme generation involves making sense of your list of carefully developed codes and clustering or combining codes to construct multifaceted and meaningful patterns that answer your research question. Phase 3 of reflexive thematic analysis (TA)—initial theme generation—continues the engagement and active processes of the previous phases, taking you deeper into analysis and understanding, but it is not your endpoint.

https://doi.org/10.1037/0000238-004
*Essentials of Thematic Analysis*, by G. Terry and N. Hayfield

In some ways, theme generation is a relatively straightforward task, with lots of strategies and processes you can use to support the construction of high-quality themes, and we will be detailing some of these in this chapter. Performing a TA is a craft skill (like all qualitative research skills); it is something learned by doing. You get better each time you do it and as you receive support and guidance from supervisors and mentors. We have found in workshops that once people have the opportunity to practice, they can quickly see how the process works for them.

Good themes capture the meaningful patterns you construct across the data items (e.g., transcripts in an interview study) in your data set (i.e., a "horizontal" method of analysis), and critically, these patterns need to go beyond description. The move beyond description is achieved by developing a strong conceptual idea that holds disparate codes and data together, as well as telling the best possible story of your data to answer your research question. Your analysis involves constructing meaningful themes that are grounded in the data, using extracts of data to evidence their credibility. You might like to think of each theme as a chapter of an overall story of the data. At the end of this phase, you will likely have more themes (or chapters) than you need and only the beginnings of your analysis (a story you want to tell). Developing the conceptual core of each theme, and the overall story that your themes tell, can sometimes feel challenging and takes time, so do try not to let that create stress. As Braun and Clarke (2013) noted, it would be incredibly unlikely that there is no way of making patterns of meaning in any given data set.

Theme construction comes with potential pitfalls, and these can be more "catastrophic" than problems in other phases. It is often at this point in analysis that we are called on to help struggling TA novices (and occasionally authors of publications we review) with fairly common problems. These difficulties generally take two forms: (a) familiarization and/or coding has been rushed, leading to a poor set of resources from which to construct themes; and (b) a tendency to hold onto untenable initial themes for too long.

Rushed familiarization and/or coding is a relatively easy fix. As with any form of product assembly, without good quality "materials" (and the right tools), it is extremely difficult to create high-quality output. Our advice here is relatively simple: Be conscious as you are producing your initial themes that returning to coding (and even familiarization) is normal and ensures the quality and quantity of your materials. Remind yourself that the TA phases are not linear, they are recursive and iterative. If they have not yet provided you with the level of engagement you need, it is not a failure.

Holding on to untenable initial themes is perhaps the more complicated issue. Supporting struggling researchers sometimes involves identifying pathways to reshape or bolster weaker themes but, more commonly, involves helping practitioners to let those themes go, freeing them to build new ones. This deconstruction and reconstruction can be disheartening (threatening even), and our support here is often as much emotional as technical. When themes have been developed and even written up but do not hold together or tell a compelling story about the data set, it is not uncommon at this point for people to talk about "wasted effort." We strongly disagree with this sentiment—no effort expended on engaging with the data is ever wasted. To address this issue before it is too late, we outline the mindset we advocate for theme development: prototyping.

### Prototyping Themes

One of the key ongoing misconceptions about theme development in reflexive TA is that it is largely a once-and-for-all process. This is something we have seen among new students and more established researchers—often as they rush to present results. Within this rubric, the later phases of a TA simply tinker at the edges of something that the researcher has prematurely decided will be a fully fledged theme, doing little more than giving them additional clarity and shape—this alone is not best practice for reflexive TA. Therefore, it is helpful to think of your early themes as *prototype themes* rather than as a final set of themes. This framing highlights their tentativeness and temporariness—for us, the terms *candidate, initial,* or *prototype* themes are largely interchangeable (e.g., Braun & Clarke, 2006; see also Braun & Clarke, 2019a). It is still extremely unusual to hear or read of people describing their theme development in ways that acknowledge this temporariness or put it at the forefront of discussing how they went about TA. Even less common is reflection on the iterative construction, deconstruction, and reconstruction processes needed to produce a high-quality theme. This is at least partially to do with journal article space for authors to write in detail about their methods, but we also suspect it has to do with attachment and investment in their early themes that have been arrived at quickly or, more problematically, with a lack of understanding of what fully developed themes are and how they are arrived at within reflexive TA.

The lingering effects and power of the idea of thematic emergence discussed in Chapter 1 also play a part. Implications that themes are simply awaiting discovery within data leaves people thinking that theming will follow a linear, defined, and quickly resolving process. Within this framing, the hope that something close to a full and final theme will arise quickly from codes and coded data seems to be common. Thematic emergence, in all its various incarnations, fundamentally draws on an archaeological or excavation orientation to data, where anticipation or expectation of quick success once the "dirt" has been cleared to get to the artifacts (or themes) is not surprising. In our perspective, though, there is not any dirt to clear. It is all data. It all has the potential to tell part of the story. You are not simply minimizing your data; you are looking to tell the best possible story about them. We have found it useful to think of theme development as akin to the prototyping of a product in design, where "the goal of prototyping *isn't to finish* [emphasis added]. It is to learn about the strengths and weaknesses of an idea and to identify further direction that prototypes might take" (Brown, 2008, p. 3). Prototypes serve a similar purpose in both design and theme development—they provide an opportunity to play with different possibilities that you would expect to need further development before implementing them.

Thinking about themes like this is both liberating and rigorous. It means that the process of "testing" becomes central to theme development. Your initial themes are purposively tentative; they are opportunities to understand and engage with your data further. If the goal of developing prototype themes is not to finish, but rather to understand, the rush to finalize them is less important than your enhanced engagement with the data. So, do not over-invest in your initial themes and instead try to think of them as prototypes or candidates. If you let them move beyond "wireframe" versions too early, it can make it hard to pull them apart (practically and emotionally) if you realize that they are not working later on. Without this iterative, recursive, reflective approach, with its testing focus, it is unlikely that the themes you construct will tell the best possible story of your data or meaningfully answer the research question.

## Practicalities of Constructing Prototype Themes

In practice, through your analysis and making connections between your codes, you can produce a number of prototype themes. During coding, you produced a set of materials through your intensive engagement with the data; however, these codes are not the final product. In this phase, your codes will disappear (especially from the final report) as you shape them into themes. Further, codes are not the "evidence" you need to confirm your already developed themes, as is common in some other forms of TA (e.g., Boyatzis, 1998; Guest et al., 2012; Joffe, 2012); rather, they are building materials that are absorbed into a whole. Your codes are like the bricks, tiles, and wood you would need to build a house (your theme). Good themes answer your research question by contributing strong central organizing concepts (Braun & Clarke, 2013; Braun et al., 2018; Terry et al., 2017), which hold the codes and their data together. This central organizing concept is formulated by the researcher and helps them determine what story the theme tells and whether codes fit within its remit or not. We move now to discuss the two key ways in which themes are constructed from codes before exploring the idea of a central organizing concept in more depth.

Constructing themes from your codes is an active process with two primary pathways: (a) clustering and (b) promoting. In both cases, the analyst uses the resources that have been produced in the first two phases (e.g., the data, familiarization notes, list of codes, knowledge they bring to the analysis) and deliberately shapes them. This task involves taking multiple individual codes that captured single ideas about extracts of data and grouping them together with the ultimate goal of producing the multifaceted, conceptually rich themes that are the hallmark of a good reflexive TA. Because the focus is on developing prototypes, this may take a few attempts, especially if you are new to the process. It is worth getting feedback from supervisors or colleagues on initial themes at this stage in the process to prevent premature locking down and overinvestment. If you are working together as a team, one way of working together is through the process of having "theme offs," whereby each member of the team develops some prototypes and presents them to the other team members. Together the team can work out the best of the options to take forward into further development.

## Clustering Codes to Construct Prototype Themes

When *clustering*, codes are grouped according to their similarity, their overlap with other codes, and additional connections that might be made intuitively at first. Clustering is the most common approach to theme building, and here, the construction or sculpting analogy is obvious. Codes that share a story about a particular aspect of the data set are identified and brought together, and the codes are relatively equal in what they bring to the developing theme. The quality of the codes becomes important to this process because the connections made need to be evident to the analyst. If codes are too broad (i.e., a single word), the meaning they capture can be lost. If an analyst is struggling here, it might indicate a need to return to the coding phase. To reiterate, this is not a "failure" on the part of the analyst, it is why we emphasize that reflexive TA is not a linear process but a recursive and iterative one.

Figure 4.1 provides an example of code clustering from the Person Centred Care (PCC) Study and shows the central organizing concept of the theme in the center, with the codes that were clustered to create the theme surrounding it. The central organizing concept here is navigating an "unfamiliar territory"—the implicit idea that people's experiences of trauma, or a new chronic condition, leave them struggling to make sense of what has happened to them, with pathways toward living well seemingly complex and unclear. This idea helps

**FIGURE 4.1. Clustering Codes**

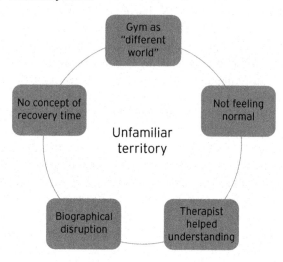

seemingly disparate codes hang together to tell one part of the story, based on an underlying conceptual foundation. Each of the codes adds something new and useful to the theme (a facet), contributing to the underlying conceptual core. This process may be something you do physically, printing your codes onto pieces of paper and cutting them out to work with, or you might also use sticky notes on a large piece of paper. Online software such as Miro and MURAL might allow you to do this on your screen and allow teams to work together when not in the same physical place. Clustering with any of these tools allows you to see the codes together, make sense of their relationships and their connections, and think about the potential for overlaps that might occur. These helpful visual processes will likely be similar when thinking about promoting a code but will identify early on that one code is more "important" than others.

## Promoting Codes to Construct Prototype Themes

*Promoting* a code recognizes that some codes might be prevalent and rich enough that they could have a central organizing concept of their own and are therefore important enough to be "promoted" from code to candidate theme. You might decide that these promoted codes capture a meaningful pattern across the data set (often evidencing this by being repeated) and share a key conceptual idea with other less dominant codes, which could then accumulate around the promoted code. Sometimes, promoted codes are latent—so the conceptual work that went into the production of their labeling has a greater payoff later in the process. Other times they are semantic codes that are extremely prevalent, having been repeated a number of times, and that capture a meaningful pattern, which other codes enable you to build on. The difference between promoting and clustering is that, in clustering, all the codes have roughly "equal weight" in what they contribute to the central organizing concept, whereas in promotion, one code is dominant and serves as the starting point of the key conceptual idea. Therefore, in promoting codes, the other codes serve to bolster and add depth, but the theme gravitates around the promoted code.

As with all reflexive TA, promoting a code involves the analyst's interpretation and discretion. Because the theme is not permanent or final and only a prototype, it is just one possibility. It is important not to promote codes too early because you risk losing useful analytic insight that comes from a thorough, unconstrained coding process. An example of promotion in the PCC Study might be the researcher having coded some data specifically with an "unfamiliar territory" code. They might have recognized the richness of this code, and the insight that occurred in the coding process was enough that this code had a central organizing concept similar to the one described earlier. The researcher might then look for other codes with similar ideas or that add something and then "attach" these codes to the promoted code (see Figure 4.2, which shows the code that was promoted to a theme in the center and the other codes that were also brought in as the theme was developed surrounding it).

Codes that are single faceted and less rich are nonetheless an important part of the data and can easily be subsumed into the promoted code's remit

**FIGURE 4.2. Promoting a Code**

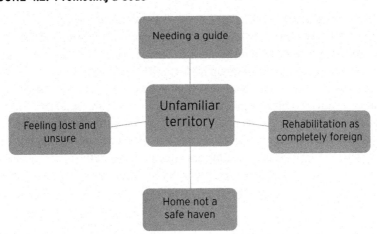

to help confirm the value of the promoted code, shifting it from simply a code to a theme, hence changing its status. In the earlier case, the code "feeling lost and unsure" adds a layer to the promoted "unfamiliar territory" code because it fits within the notion of having to navigate through a new, unfamiliar landscape. In other words, the promoted code has a central organizing concept that "captures" the other codes without losing anything of itself. The ability to promote a code speaks to the quality of the coding process, with a level of depth that is not always typical. Having discussed two potential routes for moving from codes to themes, we now elaborate on the idea of a central organizing concept.

## Themes and Central Organizing Concepts

In some descriptions of "thematic analysis" (e.g., Buetow, 2010), there is the suggestion that themes are about the simple recurrence of ideas within a data set. While this can be true, this (commonplace) framing tends to limit theme construction to the semantic similarities of codes rather than their more latent, conceptual relationship to one another. A good quality theme in reflexive TA will capture those elements of the data set that are interesting and relevant to the research question, but contributing codes may not necessarily have much semantic similarity with other codes. So, while one might have coded at the semantic level, the next steps of theme development need to go beneath the surface to the conceptual—even if just to make sense of where the connections are and draw out a central organizing concept that relates to the research question. The process involves thoughtful engagement with the meanings inscribed into the codes and ensuring that your analysis can be evidenced from the data through your knowledge of it and the resources you have created.

*Theme or Bucket?* In writing about reflexive TA, we, along with Braun and Clarke (2016; Braun et al., 2018), have distinguished between themes and domain summaries. The latter group has been described by one of Victoria's students (enthusiastically taken up by us!) as "bucket themes."

*Themes* within reflexive TA are rich, multifaceted patterns of shared meaning situated around a central organizing concept. They capture variability within a data set without being too broad, clustering data and meaning in ways that are not always immediately obvious (hence the work needed to construct them!). They often refer to something more conceptual beneath the data, clearly conveyed when the researcher tells the story of the data set. It should become straightforward, as analysis develops, to write a coherent paragraph about a theme, exploring its boundaries and central organizing concept. Their titles are also detailed and capture the core meaning of the theme.

*Domain summaries* are much simpler and often broad groupings of data built around single, "obvious" ideas that could easily preexist before analysis. They are topic based or categorical in nature, often indistinguishable from research and/or data generation questions. For instance, some researchers ask questions about "barriers" to and "facilitators" for a given phenomenon, and then their analysis produces a "theme" with this exact title. They contain diversity that cannot easily cluster, and it would be difficult to write much beyond their (disjointed) alignment with a topic. Many qualitative methodologists think of domain summaries as partially developed themes. It can often be easy to "spot" domain summaries because they generally have one-word titles that allow for an overly broad scope (e.g., "Choice," "Identity," or "Anti-Feminist Ideas"). These miss the key idea of specifically what about that topic area has been made sense of during analysis and is of interest to the reader (we find "what about . . . ?" a useful question to ask of our themes to determine that they have moved beyond domain summaries). Domain summaries are common and perfectly appropriate in some forms of qualitative analysis but do not fit with the core values of reflexive TA.

One analogy used by Braun and Clarke (2016) to describe the overall process of theme construction is baking a cake. Another colleague of Gareth's, when describing TA to a new student, spoke about building a meal from your pantry. In both cake and meal analogies, the pantry (your data set) contains a mixture of various kinds of ingredients and elements (codes) that may or may not be useful depending on what you are trying to do. It is also worth noting that the pantry has been filled by someone else (your participants). If someone conceptualizes the pantry in a categorical way, they might be able to order it along various lines (dry baking goods, tinned vegetables, sauces, spreads, nuts, and seeds).

For many people, this kind of ordering is the sum total of their thematic construction, is useful to a certain point, and might be exactly what you need. Indeed, in some forms of qualitative analysis, organizing the codes (or items in the pantry) into categories could be sufficient. However, in TA terms, categorization is the lowest level of thematic construction available (Braun & Clarke, 2016; Sandelowski & Leeman, 2012). To categorize text requires minimal interpretation. In reflexive TA, the aim is to move beyond simply categorizing and to offer instead a meaningful discussion of how you have interpreted an aspect of a data set. In contrast, in the creating a cake or meal analogy, thematic construction involves taking items that might appear categorically disparate but make total sense at the deeper level of meal coherence and flavor combinations. For instance, who would have guessed that zucchini could work in a chocolate cake? As an independent component, it appears quite disparate from the process of baking a sweet dessert, but what they bring to moistness, mouthfeel, and flavor is extraordinary. The same should be true of themes; it is not always or only the obvious code connections you should look to develop. Furthermore, confidence that your combinations of codes "work" is something that needs to be learned (through experience, through identification of ingredient value via coding and referring back to your familiarization notes).

Themes thus become more than the sum of their parts through the combination of various "ingredients from the pantry" (the data) in ways that produce a high-quality meal (the theme). Importantly, although there are shared ingredients available, the tastes of the person cooking, the experience of the cook, and the needs of those dining will result in different meal possibilities and quality. One person may use a set of ingredients and produce Vietnamese cuisine; another might use a few more ingredients, drop others, and produce a Colombian-style meal. The same is true of themes. The researcher (the cook), their research question (their family meal schedule), their underlying philosophical direction (cuisine style) produce recognizable but still different themes (meals) from the data (the pantry). This is a strength of reflexive TA and a way of thinking about themes beyond the categorical (whether or not the ingredients are all in a tin together). This does mean that the same data are potentially open to different interpretations. However, this is not problematic but rather is a key feature of reflexive TA. What is critical is that your themes are evidenced in the data—hence, in your write-up, you will partly be aiming to convince the reader that your interpretation of the data is credible. You do so by providing extracts from the data set alongside your analytic narrative, which is, in effect, you showing your interpretation of the data.

It would be good at this point to start compiling the codes and their data in separate documents or as nodes in Computer-Assisted Qualitative Data Analysis Software (if you have not already done so). This way, the testing processes that make up Phase 4 of reflexive analysis can be prepared for. However, it is useful in this phase as well because it can highlight the relationships between codes more clearly. To return to the pantry analogy, it is like keeping a record of an experimental meal, so you can try it out again to see whether it works. With all the data in one place, you can begin to make connections and clarify your decision making.

At this early stage, when you have a number of prototype themes to work with, it might be worthwhile using a tool such as a thematic map or thematic table to get a better sense of how different themes might (or might not) work with one another. These tools provide a mechanism to assess thematic boundaries (inclusion or exclusion), potential overlap, relationships, and contributions to an overall story of the data. Thematic maps provide a visual representation of the data clusters you have produced and can give different insights from simply looking at spreadsheets or documents filled with words. This is where software tools like Miro or a physical tool like post-it notes can come into their own. They can allow you to map the contours of your themes and see where there is a risk of overlap or how strongly codes "hang" around a central organizing concept. The example we have provided (see Figure 4.3) comes from the PCC Study and highlights the prototype themes for that study. The overarching prototype theme is shown in the box at the top, with themes shown in the other boxes. This was the same thematic map that the coauthors of the paper (Gareth and his colleague Nicola Kayes) used to discuss the prototype themes and their value for telling the story of the data.

Within this project, there were a large number of prototype themes (around seven) with various relationships between them identified. What is evident in this map is the quite bifurcated approach to analysis—there is a clear split between the themes associated with "valued care" and the themes associated with "systems-centered" or "clinician-centered" practices. This is not ideal because conceptually rich themes tend to be multifaceted—in other words, they should move beyond simple polarization of good and bad or barriers and facilitators, which are somewhat categorical rather than conceptual. This bifurcation likely occurred because of Gareth's newness to rehabilitation as a discipline and to his preliminary reading in this space. Also, the interviewers in many of these projects tended to ask questions that related to

**FIGURE 4.3. Thematic Map of Prototype Themes for the Person Centred Care Study**

*Note.* HCPs = health care practitioners.

valued and less helpful care. This highlights an earlier point that good themes should move beyond the scope of the interview questions, transcending rather than matching them.

Thematic tables do something similar to thematic maps in that they allow researchers to see their prototype themes in relation to one another and the codes that were used to build them. In Table 4.1, we use codes from gay and bisexual men's responses to the Body Hair Removal and Alteration (BHRA) survey to build prototype themes (note this is a constrained view of a thematic table because it does not contain codes and so forth that you might include on a large piece of butcher paper). Tables like this provide a less visualized expression of a data set than a thematic map, missing some of their more "relational" features, such as theme and subtheme connections, though they are useful for highlighting overlap and direct comparisons.

Three prototype themes were generated from the BHRA data. With the codes lying directly below the titles, it makes clear how closely, or loosely, the clusters of codes are to their central organizing concepts. The first two themes relate to grooming and the implications of new grooming expectations for men (see Terry & Braun, 2016), which seem much more intense for gay and bisexual men than for heterosexual men—what has been described as an appearance potent (Jankowski et al., 2014). The third theme relates to the exception to this grooming mandate: gay men who like (indeed, love) body hair and for whom body hair forms a significant aspect of their sexual

**TABLE 4.1. A Thematic Table to Show the Codes That Were Clustered to Develop Themes in the Gay and Bisexual Men Hair Removal Study**

| Theme 1: Grooming as essential task | Theme 2: Grooming enhances sexual capital | Theme 3: Bears have hair and don't care |
|---|---|---|
| • Location, location, location<br>• Hair growth undermines mental health<br>• Permanent removal important<br>• Grooming rituals as pleasurable<br>• Maturing bodies means more maintenance<br>• Male hairless ideal<br>• Body hair as oppressive<br>• Grooming normalized<br>• Regular maintenance needed | • Removal is about the look<br>• Grooming is sexually motivated<br>• Hair removal is invisible except for partners<br>• Maintenance increases desirability<br>• Removal emphasizes genitals<br>• Oral sex is better<br>• Removal as sexualized or erotic activity<br>• Enhances features of body<br>• "Younger" look is attractive | • Love my hairy body<br>• Bear subculture has different norms<br>• Hair important to bear identity<br>• Hair adds to attractiveness<br>• Allover hair is masculine<br>• Hairy man who likes hairy men<br>• Not interested in grooming body<br>• Hairy ideal<br>• Raw and natural is desirable |

identity—these men are often called "Bears" (Moskowitz et al., 2013). While we initially entitled this "Bears have hair and don't care," it was a tentative title because even in setting it up, we recognized that Bears do, in fact, care—it is a significant feature of their identity. However, the title initially acted as a "good enough" placeholder. This is something to keep in mind: You do not need creative, clever, or carefully developed titles for your themes at this point because they are tentative. Keeping them loose and even "buckety" (like a domain summary title) is useful to remind you that the process of theming is far from complete.

## PHASE 4: DEVELOPING AND REVIEWING THEMES

Once you have a group of candidate themes to work with, reviewing and development (Phase 4) can begin. Due to the emphasis on thematic emergence in many people's minds, this can often be another phase that gets set aside or is undercooked. But like familiarization, it is quickly obvious that someone has omitted this phase when reading their work—the themes tend toward being buckety, and there is often a lot of conceptual overlap. This crucial phase allows a researcher to reconnect the prototype themes to the collated data and wider data set to ensure the story that is being told has not drifted too far into interpretation beyond what you can evidence in the data (i.e., interpretation is a balance where analysis does need to be grounded in the data rather than becoming entirely speculative) and to actively explore the prototypes and their value.

As with all good design, the testing and further development process is what enhances the final product. If you built a motorway overpass without assessing the merits of various designs and testing them out (using Computer-Aided Design software to virtually model the designs), there would be a good chance the final product could be overpriced and inefficient (and worse, it could be dangerous). While the risks of not testing your themes and then developing them further to enhance robustness are not as profound as a failing motorway overpass, the same principle applies—untested themes are unlikely to hold up well. Experience doing TA and other forms of qualitative research can reduce their risk of "failure," but it is not a guarantee, so the reviewing and development phase is something we advise TA practitioners to do, no matter their experience. In saying that, the more experience one has, the more the processes of theme prototyping and reviewing and developing can blur together. For newer researchers, though, it is worth making them clear and distinct phases.

The type of end-product solution that review and development seek to provide is (a) the best of various candidate themes developed through all the phases, (b) the best "shape" for the developed themes based on your data, and (c) the combinations of these themes that tell the best story of the data. If you only grab at the earliest (and obvious) themes (which will often end up being categories or domain summaries rather than conceptually rich themes), you will never be able to tell the best possible story that can be produced at the intersection of your analytic insight and interpretation, your research question, and the data you have collected. Generating themes with the intention of creating options or possibilities to be tested and then further developing them is one of the hallmarks of reflexive TA. Review and development are central to this process and help ensure quality control.

This is the "pressure testing" phase, which means asking a number of questions. Have you constructed something that is a product of cherry-picking data or that is simply a great idea that is not thematic (anecdotalism) or something that does not answer your research question? Reviewing is essential to answer these questions and give a strong sense of the stability of your themes. To do so, you will review at two levels: your coded data and the overall data set. During these dual processes, holding on to your prototypes only lightly is essential. In some cases, the reviewing process confirms that your candidate themes are of high quality and may only need small developmental tweaks, or none at all, though this is rare.

Going back to your coded data (the data associated with your codes that you will often have collated within a single document) and the overall data set from which you developed your codes, allows you to check that each prototype works in relation to the research question and the data themselves and determine whether there are different ways the data could be understood. Thematic tables are one tool that can give some useful insight into the process. In Table 4.2, we have reproduced some of the codes and prototype themes for the PCC Study as a table using three of the themes: a difficult new reality, "doctators" (a combination of the words *doctor* and *dictator*), and health care professionals as guides.

With the table of codes acting as a placeholder, you can see some of the distinctiveness of the first theme. It is rich, multifaceted, and distinctive. Although there is some room to work it up, develop it, and certainly see where it fits within the wider story, it shows all the indications of a "good" theme. When making these assessments, it is worthwhile asking yourselves questions about the prototypes. Braun and Clarke (2012) and Braun et al. (2015) provided some examples of the kinds of things you can ask about your prototypes:

- Is this more than just a code? Is it a theme in that multiple codes are able to cluster around its central organizing concept?

- What does this prototype tell us about the data set and our research question?

**TABLE 4.2. A Thematic Table to Show the Codes That Were Clustered to Develop Themes in the Person Centred Care Study**

| Theme 1: A difficult new reality | Theme 2: "Doctators" | Theme 3: Health care professionals as guides |
|---|---|---|
| • In need of navigation<br>• The big unknown<br>• Identity in flux<br>• New terrain needs guides<br>• Who am I now?<br>• Biographical disruption<br>• Finding pathways to improvement<br>• The gym landscape as foreign<br>• Giving shape to new life<br>• Bewildered and disoriented<br>• Where is information found? | • Doctors not believing her<br>• Making decisions without consulting<br>• A body not a person<br>• Self-advocacy irritating clinicians<br>• No relationship<br>• Treating condition not the person<br>• Not answering questions<br>• Consent processes not always clear | • Provides a framework to understand new life<br>• Guidance is key<br>• Talking about possible trajectories<br>• Relationship is central to understanding<br>• Needs of the client drive direction of treatment<br>• Always checking in with client<br>• Dynamic consent<br>• Takes the whole person into consideration |

- What does this prototype theme include and exclude? What are its boundaries? Are those boundaries permeable (is there overlap with other themes)?

- How much data are there to support this prototype? Would too much need to be made of too little? Are there good exemplars of data evident that could be used?

- How broad is the theme? Does it contain a strong central organizing concept, or are the data too diverse, suggesting it is a domain summary rather than a theme?

When asking these questions of the second two themes in the thematic table, it became obvious that these were not distinct entities but rather two sides of the same conceptual coin. In other words, being a doctator was the negative expression of a health care provider who might otherwise be a guide. When looking at the codes and then the data for these two themes, it became apparent that they were referring to a concept that went beneath the surface of Gareth's initial reading. They both spoke to a relational orientation to care valued by participants that was absent in some cases and present in others. Unlike "barriers" and "facilitators," this did not just collapse the two ideas together into a "theme" but, rather, produced something meaningful that captured both concepts.

This same feature was apparent across the whole initial analysis, as already identified in the previous phases of a bifurcated set of themes, with one aligned with "good care" and the other with "indifferent care." By referring to the data within each of the seven prototypes and the data set overall, something deeper and useful became evident, which can be seen within the final thematic map in Figure 4.4.

The analytic insight of avoiding the simplistic, bifurcated reading of the data meant that themes were collapsed from seven to four. All care described and valued existed within the difficult new reality of the patients, with three key types of practice described, which made person-centered care come to full fruition and benefit: (a) a relational orientation to care, (b) trust being understood as a type of capital or currency that enabled better care if it was attained and built up, and (c) health care practitioners as supporting capability and efficacy within their patients. This story was simpler but had more richness than the one told by the original prototypes. In this case, one insight from the reviewing and developing process for a single theme had ramifications for a number of the prototypes. The final thematic map in Figure 4.4 was then "tested out" in conferences and conversations among the research team and beyond and was used to help think through the next phases of the analysis. This use of "initial" and "final" maps is a useful process and will likely involve more than two maps—in fact, for this project, we had four.

The hair removal data involved a much less dramatic shift from prototype to final themes than the PCC data. We were happy with the first two

**FIGURE 4.4. Final Thematic Map for the Person Centred Care Study**

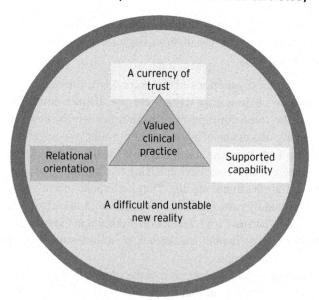

themes and their alignment with the data from all men in the wider survey (see Terry & Braun, 2016). As already noted, it was the looseness of the "Bears have hair and don't care" theme that needed tightening. In this case, it was less about the data within the theme than how the theme fitted with the whole data set. It was evident that grooming (or not) was an identity issue for all the men (rather than a particular subculture), and this offered more interpretive value than the explicit focus on the group of men who preferred hairy bodies. This theme was then developed as a way of discussing the wider "mainstream" of gay and bisexual men's body hair removal, as well as the exceptions to the "rules." A subtheme of "Bears care about hair" could then be added to the overall discussion of the final theme, with the central organizing concept of this subtheme relating to that of the main theme.

During the review process, you can also be thinking about the relationship between themes and how best to tell the story of your data. You do not necessarily have to include subthemes, but they can be useful because relationships not only happen between themes but also within themes. Sometimes students struggle to differentiate between themes and subthemes, so we provide a brief definition here. *Themes* capture the overarching story of the data set, with their own central organizing concept. There need to be clear boundaries between these themes—in other words, themes should be distinctive from each other rather than overlapping. *Subthemes* exist within themes, and while they contain their own central organizing concept and title, this operates both in relation to the primary theme and any other subthemes within the primary theme. One element that is often misunderstood is how to report subthemes—many people tend to let them "dominate" the theme, sometimes so much so that the main theme is hard to identify because it has fragmented and the overall focus has been lost. You might like to think of subthemes as helping you structure your analysis without leading or dominating it.

Determining when to stop the reviewing and development phase can also be a difficult decision but one that the researcher makes, not one defined by the data themselves. After all, themes are the sculptures you have carved from the data set, not entities you find in the data. Decisions about when to finish are based on criteria that are largely pragmatic—like those of a sculptor or woodcarver or, to return to the cooking analogy, the chef. How much improvement will you make by continuing to whittle away at your themes? Are they telling a great story about your data set already? What sorts of external deadlines do you have? Are you procrastinating? It is worth remembering that this is not the final phase of the analytical process, and refinement will continue beyond this phase. In fact, the next phase is often the one in which the researcher fully realizes the potential of a theme and highlights in great detail its boundaries and strengths. In the meantime, "taste testing" your themes (and even getting others to taste them with you) can help you decide readiness—you can always make something better, but is it sufficient? Are your deadlines (dinnertime!) upon you? We should also point out that by the time Phase 4 has been completed, your engagement with the data will be such that you will be brimming with ideas and possibilities. One student of Gareth's commented recently that he felt like he was ready to explode and just wanted to get his thoughts onto paper.

## PHASE 5: NAMING AND DEFINING THEMES

By Phase 5, you will have done a lot of work. You have constructed a group of themes and potentially subthemes that support the structure of each of your themes. The tendency here might be to think that because of all this work, you can relax. However, now is not the time to ease off—the upcoming explosion of writing activity needs to be clearly directed. We often associate this phase with creativity and those moments you have when waking up with an idea or when having a shower or taking a walk—things consolidate in your head and feel like inspiration or even revelation. This is perhaps unsurprising, given how immersed you are in your analysis by this time. However, these moments do not come from the ether. They are a product of previous effort and engagement and still involve the work of transferring, of shuffling, of rethinking, and, most important, of still being willing to recognize that things can still change or not do what you expect them to do. It is at this point in the analysis that the story of the analytic narrative will be produced. This phase is made up of two components that are strongly related: producing thematic definitions and naming your themes.

### Writing Theme Definitions

We are big advocates of thematic definitions. These are essentially extended versions of a theme's central organizing concepts and are useful for those doing a TA, as well as for mentors and supervisors who might be supporting the primary researcher. Theme definitions act as (a) a way to help refine themes further; (b) confirmation that your themes have the necessary conceptual and story-telling depth to be able to write a paragraph or more about your themes without resulting in so much text or digression, which would indicate that there may be too much content for a coherent theme; and (c) a means to allow the relational shape and overall story of your themes to become clearer to you than they previously were. This is where the analysis and theme development begin to become written interpretation, taking on features of clarity, precision, and cohesion. In Exhibit 4.1, we have taken one of the themes for the PCC Study and provided an example of a thematic definition.

The definition in Exhibit 4.1 provides a level of depth and detail regarding the theme of relational orientation to care and acts as a "chapter summary" or abstract for this theme but can also stand alone. Theme definitions can help determine whether a theme is thin or thick (whether you are making too much of too little or not) or whether a theme contains too many divergent ideas (in which case you may get a sense that your theme is not cohering around the central organizing concept and is perhaps becoming fragmented). If you are unable to provide a definition with similar levels of detail to Exhibit 4.1, it is likely that your theme is not rich enough or that the central organizing concept is weak. Another possibility is that the theme being described could end up being a subtheme rather than a theme and should be "demoted" or merged into another theme. However, if you cannot capture the key ideas concisely and distinctly, it may be that some content could be let go, or the theme could be split into subthemes or even potentially separate themes. What can be gleaned from these possibilities is that being willing to let things go is still important. We keep repeating this like a mantra because it has proven so central to the successful development of high-quality themes.

We have found thematic definitions extremely helpful when working with colleagues and our students. These thematic definitions provide an opportunity to discuss the detail of a TA, without having to provide the whole analysis and serve as an opportunity for supervisors (and colleagues) to "intervene" if things do not seem to be working—to bolster from their own readings of the

**EXHIBIT 4.1. A Thematic Definition for the Person Centred Care Study**

**Relational Orientation in Care**

This theme identifies that the therapeutic relationship and "success" with a client move beyond a set of tasks (and sometimes even initial clinical outcomes), treating the relationship as a priority. The therapeutic relationship is not then understood as a welcome addition to rehabilitation, but the basis of it. Participants often identified that what seems to be a dead end of improvement in the physical sphere can result in unacknowledged possibilities across others. Practitioners who were considered "good" by participants often engaged with the client in ways that moved beyond the task or program, motivating them through the relationship built up between them. In contrast, "doctators" treated their clients as a set of tasks or parts of a body that needed to be repaired. Depth of relationship (or perception of such) had the potential to enable greater engagement, high levels of motivation, and a willingness to participate in tasks that seemed difficult or mundane.

data; and to check for resonance and connections to literature and data before the researchers commit to the final efforts of writing. Further, the theme definitions are the start of the writing up, where you work out your structure and a place to start your narrative rather than facing the distress of a blank document in Word. Although Phase 6 is where writing begins in earnest, it is the products of each phase that enable the depth and ease of interpretation and writing associated with that final phase.

## Naming Themes

As discussed earlier, it is common for themes to have working titles, especially at the prototyping stage of development. These are generally just something to group your codes and data under and should remain tentative—because, again, premature naming can constrain the willingness to deconstruct a theme that is not working. However, it is in Phase 5 that the final name of the theme can be generated and working titles can give way to creative energy and crafting. In Exhibit 4.2, we have provided theme names and subtheme names for the PCC project.

We both like engaging, interesting titles for theme names and enjoy the process of developing these. We also like "grounding" the theme name in our participants' words, which is its own form of creativity, and they all form a part of the theme name. Overall, a good theme name should capture something about the central organizing concept of a theme, which is why this part of the phase comes after producing thematic definitions and why some theme names may need to be a little lengthy on occasion. Theme names should give a clear indication of the theme's content and prime the reader for the analysis, acting as a signpost for the story being told. In Exhibit 4.2, the theme of "a difficult and unstable new reality" is tied to the subtheme of the

---

**EXHIBIT 4.2. Theme and Subtheme Names for the Person Centred Care Study**

*Theme 1:* "So there's all this danger, you know, you don't sort of realize until you get home"—a difficult and unstable new reality

*Subthemes:* (a) wanting to die, (b) problems adapting, (c) home as a source of danger

*Theme 2:* "I mean I've only known them all of 2 weeks, but you'd swear I'd known them for 6 months"—relational orientation in care

*Subthemes:* (a) relationship as priority, (b) guides through the new reality, (c) having a real relationship

*Theme 3:* "I think it's important to gain the faith of the person that you are dealing with"—a currency of trust.

*Subthemes:* (a) building trust, (b) sustaining trust, (c) the transferability of trust "home as a source of danger" through a quotation. The quotation comes from a participant whose child had experienced a traumatic brain injury and, due to behavioral changes and a lack of impulse control, was often getting into trouble in the previously safe space of the family home. These sorts of connections are extremely useful for conference presentations, where there is much less scope to discuss a theme in great detail, but a pithy quotation and title can help tell the story.

At the end of this phase, you have all the raw (and refined) material you need to make writing a pleasurable, even fun activity. Through multiple levels of engagement with the data, you (and perhaps colleagues you are working with) will have a better sense of them than anybody else. At the end of this phase, you will have a story to tell. At the final part of the phase, collecting data extracts that fit well with your theme name and definition is an important step. Compelling extracts of data that speak to the kinds of issues you want to discuss are important. If you are planning on using your sub-themes to help structure the writing of your themes, extracts that tap into the central organizing concept of each subtheme are useful to have before you begin writing the report—the final phase of TA.

In this chapter, we discussed the three phases of reflexive TA that are essential to theme construction. We identified the importance of beginning with a pool of well-developed resources from familiarization and coding, which act as the components you will need to build your themes. We emphasized that during these phases, you engage at an even deeper level with the data than during familiarization and coding through the production of a number of prototype themes, testing them through a review and development phase and, then, once you have decided on your themes, naming and defining them. All these phases contribute to the development of strong, conceptually rich themes that move beyond simple description or summary of the data and provide you with plenty of material to help direct and structure your writing processes.

# 5 REPORTING YOUR RESEARCH AND WRITING THE RESULTS

The emphasis on reflexivity and flexibility within reflexive thematic analysis (TA) means that there are some specific considerations researchers need to address when producing research reports. We draw on the American Psychological Association (APA) reporting standards (Levitt et al., 2018) to discuss how your write-up can be aligned with the journal article reporting standards (JARS) for qualitative research when producing written reports, including journal papers. However, you will need to consider the requirements of your discipline or subdiscipline and specific journals in making your decision, and it also might be worth considering whether these requirements need to be debated. Many journals rely on particularly positivist structures for articles that are more traditionally associated with quantitative reports. However, this is changing as more and more journals recognize the variations in style that different theoretical perspectives might have—particularly the differences between structures that make sense for qualitative versus quantitative research.

Levitt et al. (2018) referred to two forms of methodological integrity: (a) *fidelity to the subject matter* relates to how the researcher connects with or conceptualizes their data, and (b) *utility in achieving research goals* relates

https://doi.org/10.1037/0000238-005
*Essentials of Thematic Analysis*, by G. Terry and N. Hayfield

to the design and methods and how well they are suited to the aims and research question (see Levitt et al., 2018, p. 33; Levitt et al., 2017, p. 10). In our minds, the methodological integrity of your work is inherent to writing your report and is evident in this chapter's guidelines and throughout the rest of the book. Further, writing the report is the final phase of a reflexive TA. It is still part of the process of doing analysis, and this needs to be kept in mind throughout. Having gathered the data extracts you think are most salient to your analysis, you will write up your themes in ways that enhance and develop the work you have done in previous phases, contextualizing them by bringing the analysis into "conversation" with the sociocultural and academic context through the use of literature. All this involves a return to the fundamentals of good research practice, reminding yourself of what drew you to the research, what theory or theories defined your research, and the way you used various methods to help construct your final output, whether it be dissertation, thesis, journal article, book chapter, or report.

## WRITING YOUR INTRODUCTION

Whatever your methodology or theoretical orientation, it is important that your introduction includes a discussion of the extant literature. This should be presented so that the reader has a strong sense of what is already known about your topic and what is missing from our knowledge of it or where that knowledge needs refining. The reader needs to know the rationale for your study and to understand if there is a particular type of research problem you are trying to solve. Therefore, the researcher's aim in the introduction is often to make a convincing argument about the existence of a knowledge gap and how your TA research will make a worthy contribution to filling it or how your research is likely to bring something of value. We also encourage researchers to explicitly state their aims and research question(s) so that these are clear from the outset.

## WRITING THE METHOD FOR TA

The method section is particularly pertinent for TA practitioners. TA's theoretical flexibility means that it is especially necessary to state clearly the choices you made and the processes you followed in your analysis (see Chapters 1, 3, and 4). We suspect that many published articles skim over the details of their methods and methodologies due to the constraints of journal word limits, but we encourage authors to (concisely) include as much detail as possible.

Understanding the "why" of a method is often more important than the "how." Nonetheless, we have often found it useful to think about reporting methods in a way that aims to give the reader sufficient information to understand both why you chose this method and to know enough about how you used the method to be able to (in theory) replicate your research because this can ensure that your processes are clear. Further, the results of a paper should reflect your theoretical orientations and descriptions of process. Make clear all the choices you made regarding the "type" of TA you have done and the methodological package you created. We have argued that these are extremely important for doing a TA (see Chapter 1), and returning to these choices in the write-up is just as key to good research practice. Is the TA you have done realist or relativist or something in between? (See Chapter 6 for examples of these variations.) Did you take an experiential or critical approach? Did you approach the data inductively or deductively or a bit of both? Did you code semantically or latently or use a mixture of these? We discuss this in more detail later because it is so crucial. The method section is not just a tick box exercise—people do read them.

## Procedure and Participants

Many forms of data collection are suitable for TA (see Chapter 2), and we recommend that the method section includes the rationale for your choices, situated in relation to the topic, your research question(s), and perhaps your participant group—with supporting citations—ordered according to journal prescriptions. Mention how your research materials were developed (e.g., how did you ascertain what questions to ask, were these piloted and with whom, were pilot responses included in the final data set, were materials further developed during the study on the basis of piloting and/or early data collection, and if so, what types of changes did you make). Tell the reader in what format data were collected (e.g., online, email, or hard copy data collection or audio recordings of face-to-face methods). Report how many interviews or focus groups took place, including where they were held or how they were conducted (e.g., Skype, telephone, online synchronous or asynchronous). For textual data, state how many responses you had (e.g., to your survey, story completion, or other data collection method). Also report the duration (e.g., the shortest and longest interview or focus group, means and ranges of the length, and perhaps average times participants spent on surveys or other textual data collection methods, if known). If you used existing data sources, state how you identified these and how many were selected for inclusion in the analysis and on what basis. Readers will want to know which authors were involved in data collection and how many researchers and participants were present. You also need to discuss what participants were asked to do and what procedures were followed. We find that the most concise way to report data collection procedures is to combine ethical considerations, materials, and procedure (e.g., participants were first asked to read an information sheet that fully informed them about the study purpose and procedures and outlined their right to withdraw and how their data would be managed; and so on).

Readers will want to know about your recruitment techniques, your participant numbers, and participant demographics (see the following paragraph)—both to contextualize data collection and give the reader a picture of who took part and therefore to whom the data and results relate (see Elliott et al., 1999). Specific inclusion or exclusion criteria should be mentioned, as should any incentives you offered participants. Include where the study was advertised and your recruitment strategies (e.g., purposive sampling, snowball sampling, aiming for a diverse or homogenous sample; see Braun & Clarke, 2013). There should also be a rationale for how many participants or data sources you aimed to include, based on qualitative guidance (e.g., Braun & Clarke, 2013; Terry et al., 2017); how you decided when to stop collecting data; and the final numbers—perhaps with some acknowledgment of the realities of recruiting people or finding materials (particularly if you did not meet your initial targets).

Be sure to describe your data sources or provide a summary of participants' demographics (e.g., age, gender, sexuality, race and ethnicity, disabilities, alongside specific characteristics of your participants relevant to your topic). In addition to this overview, also include sufficient further detail about participant demographics. For ethical reasons and to ensure the confidentiality of those who took part in your research, we suggest amalgamated demographic summaries rather than participant-by-participant reports of individuals within your sample (e.g., report $x$ number of participants were Black Caribbean, $x$ number were White British rather than P1: Black Caribbean, P2: White British). Finally, inform readers how audio and textual data were managed in preparation for analysis (e.g., how data were transcribed and by whom, including the notation system; text transferred to Word or Excel; any editing of participant responses such as removal of hesitations from participants' talk or removal of spelling and grammatical errors in textual data).

## Researcher Reflexivity

TA is a reflexive analytic method, so it is critical to indicate the researchers' positions in relation to the topic and the participants. This section is often rather brief or even missing entirely in many TA reports. At a minimum, the

JARS for qualitative research recommend that researchers indicate how their understanding of the topic and their sociodemographic characteristics might have influenced data collection and analysis. We encourage you to be specific about this. For student projects, we recommend including a reflexive statement (perhaps in the appendices) that outlines the researcher's relationship to the topic and participants (e.g., ways in which you are an insider and ways in which you are an outsider; see Hayfield & Huxley, 2015) and in what ways this impacted design, data collection, data analysis, and the final results in some depth. We have also written book chapters where we have elaborated on the reflexive elements of our research, to which we refer readers of journal articles (see, e.g., Terry et al., 2017).

## Data Analysis

While some qualitative methods come with their own set of theoretical underpinnings, this is not the case for reflexive TA (see Chapter 1, this volume, and Terry et al., 2017), so it is particularly important to state your choices explicitly. These are discussed in detail in Chapters 1 and 2, but as a brief reminder, the key dialectic choices are inductive–deductive, semantic–latent, and experiential–critical and the researchers' ontological or epistemological approach (e.g., realist, critical realist, constructionist). We often see published research where there is no explicit reference to the researchers' ontologies or epistemologies, and we consider this problematic (because of the flexibility of TA, the reader will not necessarily understand your analytic approach without this). It may also be in this section that researchers outline any theories or approaches (e.g., positioning theory, feminist approaches) that informed the research, although these could be located elsewhere in the methods or introduction (see Table 5.1).

We also urge researchers to discuss specifically how they conducted the phases of TA. Again, due to the flexibility of TA, it is useful for readers to understand how you undertook the processes in some detail. We often integrate our choices within our discussion of the processes we followed to enable us to be concise. We encourage those writing about their analysis to do so in such a way that they take ownership of their analysis by discussing who was involved during each of the phases and how these decisions were managed. This could include an outline of the order in which the phases were undertaken and in what way these were recursive—remembering that TA is not simply a recipe to be followed. Table 5.1 shows an example of a write-up from a published paper.

Braun and Clarke (2020) have written extensively about how reflexive TA is sometimes understood and reported within journals in ways that are not

**TABLE 5.1. Extract From a Data Analysis Section**

| Data analysis section | Narrative on the data analysis section |
|---|---|
| "We undertook our analysis within a critical realist ontology (Sims-Schouten et al., 2007). Critical realism treats knowledge and experience as mediated and constructed through language, while acknowledging material and social structures that generate phenomena. This analytic lens enabled us to theorize realities as existing beyond discourse, while simultaneously acknowledging the personal as thoroughly embedded in the social context. . . . All authors read and re-read transcripts, and each generated separate analytical notes. After meeting to discuss our initial impressions, all authors engaged in inductive and deductive coding in a recursive manner; after our initial coding, we returned to our codes and revised them as the coding and analytic process proceeded. We clustered codes together to identify candidate themes, to determine whether patterns were evident across most or all of the data set, and check how well these candidate themes provided an overall account of the data (see Terry et al., 2017). . . . Theme construction was iterative and consultative, with all authors coding separately, but meeting regularly throughout this process to consider our interpretations of the data and discuss the findings. All authors then discussed the two themes in detail and ensured that each theme cohered around a central organizing concept, which is the key idea that underpins the thematic explanation of the data (Terry et al., 2017). Themes and theme names were reviewed and refined following conference presentations of preliminary analysis, during further discussion, and while writing this article." | This early part of our data analysis section introduces the reader to our ontological and epistemological approach with a brief overview. We include citations to support our writing and to which readers can refer. This section also serves to inform the reader of the choice of an experiential or critical approach.<br><br>Here we start to discuss the processes of thematic analysis (TA). We make clear that all the authors were involved in the analysis. By telling the reader about our reading and rereading the transcripts, we are clarifying how the research team familiarized themselves with the data (Phase 1). We then move on to talk about Phase 2 (coding) and make clear that we did not follow the processes of TA in a linear fashion but instead revisited coding at various points. We incorporate our choices of TA within the discussion of the processes (coding was both inductive and deductive). We report how we moved from codes to themes (Phase 3) and how we reviewed themes (Phase 4). We are transparent about which of the authors were involved in the analytic process and how we shared our ideas and agreed on the final themes. While we had reviewed themes (Phase 4) earlier in the analysis, we also report on further review and consideration of theme names (Phase 5) that happened when we shared our findings with others and as we wrote the report (Phase 6). |

theoretically congruent. In particular, reports of themes emerging from the data dominate much of the published literature, as though there was only one version of analysis available from any data set (see Chapter 1). As we have discussed, the researcher(s); their positions in relation to the topic, participants, and data; and their wider approaches (e.g., other theoretical ideas they may have drawn on) all inform how the researcher arrived at the best possible story based on the data (Braun & Clarke, 2016; Braun et al., 2019). Another key issue is the tendency for some researchers to report various techniques (e.g., developing codebooks, interrater reliability) in their methods. However, such techniques are (often) based on positivist and quantitative criteria of objectivity, which do not fit with the Big-Q approach to qualitative research within which reflexive TA is embedded (Braun & Clarke, 2016).

## WRITING THE RESULTS SECTION

There is flexibility and variation in how to report a TA, and we now set out some guidance for good practice in structuring the results section. Broadly, there are two possibilities for the overall structure: (a) a results section in which you report your themes, followed by a separate discussion section that relates your findings to the literature; and (b) an integrated section of your themes and your discussion relating your themes to the literature. We tend to prefer the latter because it feels somewhat less repetitive than revisiting key ideas across more than one section and can potentially enable a more in-depth and contextualized analytic report. Levitt et al. (2018) noted that results and discussion sections can be difficult to separate because the two are intertwined, highlighting that what is important is that the relevant components are present in a manuscript. We also recommend referring back to Chapter 4 in terms of what constitutes a strong analysis before you begin writing your report. We have seen journal articles in which the authors seem to overlook various phases of a TA—in particular, the final phase of writing the report—yet producing the report is as important as any other phase. It is at this point that you are most immersed in your data, and writing up your themes serves as a real test of how well they work, which is why we see this as an important part of the analytic phases of reflexive TA. During this phase, you may have some of your most insightful ideas, so be willing to let things go and to potentially make final (meaningful) changes to your themes.

We recommend starting your results section with a brief introduction to your themes so that the reader has an overview of your analysis. This introduction could simply list your theme titles (e.g., Jowett et al., 2012), or it could also include mention of the central organizing concept and/or a sentence or two about each theme (e.g., Hayfield et al., 2019). You could also include a thematic map to show a diagrammatic representation of your themes, perhaps at the start of your results section or as an appendix. Each theme should then be presented, with theme names as the headings and subtheme names as subheadings.

We recommend that the best way to start each theme is to introduce the reader to the overarching idea or central organizing concept of the theme and its subthemes (bearing in mind that there may be many facets to a theme or subtheme). Next, ground your analysis in the data using vivid data extracts (e.g., participants' quotations or extracts of text from your secondary sources). A strong TA will include compelling and convincing data extracts. There will need to be enough extracts to demonstrate to the reader that your claims about the data are credible and to show that the pattern was evident in multiple instances across the data. Include participant codes or pseudonyms so that readers can see that you have used extracts from a range of different participants or sources. You may also want to include selective demographic information such as participant gender and age (see Exhibit 5.1) so that there is some context about each participant within the results section.

If you are using data from surveys (or other textual data methods), you will most likely incorporate multiple examples of short extracts within a sentence, which looks a little like a list. If your data are from interviews or focus groups, you may have fewer but longer quotations that look more like a block of text (and when data extracts are 30 words or more, they should be set out from the main text and indented). Exhibit 5.1 gives some examples of how this might look. These different styles occur because data from surveys are more likely to consist of shorter (and perhaps thinner) responses (that you use more of), whereas data from interviews and focus groups tend to consist of longer (and usually thicker), more in-depth detailed responses. This is not a hard-and-fast rule, and it may be that your survey data are sufficiently in-depth that they look more like interview data and that you include both shorter and longer extracts.

After introducing your overall theme and its central organizing concept and showing some data, it is crucial to incorporate analytic discussion that will contextualize your results and analysis within the existing literature. You then describe another facet of your theme, show some data, and include some further analytic narrative (see the Appendix for a list of exemplar studies using TA that include a strong results section). Be aware that data extracts do not "speak for themselves" and that simply paraphrasing what a participant has said (or saying nothing) is not the same as an analytic narrative demonstrating your interpretation of the data. When you are doing this

## EXHIBIT 5.1. Writing Examples

### Example of Multiple Short Extracts From Survey Data

From " 'It Shouldn't Stick Out From Your Bikini at the Beach': Meaning, Gender, and the Hairy/Hairless Body," by V. Braun, G. Tricklebank, and V. Clarke, 2013, *Psychology of Women Quarterly, 37*(4), pp. 482–483.

> Some simply expressed the view that what one does with one's pubic hair is personal choice and left it at that. For example, "It is a personal decision it's up to them what they do with it" (06M[19]); "Up to them. Personal preference" (34M[22]); "Only if they want to. Personal choice" (10M[37]); "It is an individual decision" (11F[37]); "Don't really care, it is up to them" (45F[no age given]); and "I don't think people should remove pubic hair unless they want to" (30F[41]). Some explicitly framed their position as a non-judgemental [sic] one: "I think people should do what they feel is right for them. I don't judge people either way" (53M[32]) and "[Pubic hair removal is] really up to them. If they think they need to then why not? It does not make any difference from my point of view" (48M[23]).

### Examples of Data Extracts From Interviews or Focus Groups

Interviews: From " 'Why Can't I Just Not Drink?' A Qualitative Study of Adults' Social Experiences of Stopping or Reducing Alcohol Consumption," by A. Bartram, J. Eliott, and S. Crabb, 2017, *Drug and Alcohol Review, 36*(4), p. 452.

> Paloma (30–34 years old) described these aspersions as hurtful, intensifying her sense of discomfort in drinking situations:
>
> > I really feel bad when someone tells me "What's wrong with you that you're not drinking?," and I'm like "Oh yeah maybe I'm wrong, maybe I shouldn't be here," or "Yeah, I'm such a boring person."
>
> To minimise their experience of stigma, participants reported developing strategies to manage their social lives while reducing their alcohol consumption.

Focus groups: From "Performance or Appearance? Young Female Sport Participants' Body Negotiations," by C. Lunde and K. H. Gattario, 2017, *Body Image, 21*, p. 85.

> These social norms added a negative component to the young women's eating and a sense of shame of eating "too much."
>
> A:  [People might say to me] "wow you take a lot of food" [and I say] "yeah, I know, I'm hungry." I don't know, but it's hard when somebody points it out.
>
> E:  You feel, like, fat, when you take that much food. And you meet someone who's like "I'm not that hungry, I'll just take a glass of water" and then you think "oh, should I really eat all this?"
>
> J:  Yeah, I sometimes take more food than the guys in my class . . . and someone [comments] "guys eat so much!" and I sit there with the same amount of food. (Group 3)
>
> The shame involved in eating large amounts of food led several of the young women to be more careful in their eating, trying to restrict the amount of food they ate at school, for instance.

analytical work, be sure to locate the theme in relation to your research question and the extant literature. There are two approaches to writing around extracts: (a) using data *illustratively*, where your writing and the "connective tissue" between your analytic points are summed up with the use of an extract; and (b) using data *analytically*, where the data serve as a platform from which to discuss the meaning making that is present in the text and to offer analytic insights that speak specifically to this particular data extract. It is much more common for people to use the first approach, but the second approach is useful, especially when analyzing data using a relativist version of reflexive TA (see Chapters 1 and 6).

The proportion of data extracts to analytic narrative across the theme will be informed partly by whether you combine or separate the results and discussion and by your theoretical and epistemological approaches. Too few quotations can suggest that there are insufficient data to evidence your theme convincingly, whereas too many quotations can be indicative of an under-developed analysis that would benefit from further analytic discussion. As a loose guideline, there should be a roughly 50:50 split between data extracts and analytic narrative (e.g., your discussion that tells the reader how you have made sense of the data and leads them through the theme; Braun & Clarke, 2006, 2012). Higher proportions of analytic narrative may be necessary in some circumstances, for example, if you are combining results and discussion sections. How many data extracts you include will also vary depending on your theoretical and epistemological approaches, which in themselves shape the style of analytic report (see, for example, separate results and discussion sections in a realist TA reported by Williams et al., 2019, in contrast with a combined results and discussion section of a social constructionist TA, informed by discourse analysis and positioning theory, reported by Bartram et al., 2019). In whatever way you report your results, include data extracts and a discussion that clearly articulates your analytical thinking. We also recommend that you avoid ending a theme on a participant quotation and instead finish by briefly summing up the theme and perhaps signposting to the next theme.

Overall, when writing the manuscript, it is important that the reader has a clear sense of the quality of your research. In addition to the recent APA guidelines, there are a number of published papers that discuss sets of criteria to use when evaluating qualitative research, and there are many debates about which are the most appropriate and whether one set of guidelines is suited to all forms of qualitative research. While there are too many separate lists of guidelines and too many debates about them for us to provide full details for readers in this book, you may find different sets of criteria useful to consider when evaluating the quality of your research project (e.g., Elliott et al., 1999; Parker, 2004; Terry et al., 2017; Tracy, 2010; Yardley, 2000).

However, it is important to recognize that these criteria should never be used prescriptively for qualitative research. We recommend that they act as guides only, offering insight into areas where researchers have not considered all the possibilities of their work and writing. There has been a tendency for decades for reviewers, editors, and publishers to impose these criteria on authors for papers to be accepted. Checklists, such as the Consolidated Criteria for Reporting Qualitative Research, were originally designed by generating items from the most frequently included items in other checklists (Tong et al., 2007) and thus suffer the same blind spots and assumptions of those original checklists (see Barbour, 2001, for a useful critique of these). Certainly, assumptions about data collection methods (only mentioning interviews) and needing to refer to rigor checks such as saturation are limiting and only reify the status of mechanisms that are not necessarily important or helpful (Braun & Clarke, 2019b). Use these guides to support your thinking, not constrain your ideas of what "counts" as quality reporting of qualitative research.

In this chapter, we explored writing up your analysis and highlighted how this phase is part of the analytic process. When writing your results, you have a final opportunity to review and refine your analysis as you make connections to existing literature and consider the methodological integrity of your research. We included some tips and examples of what readers might expect from a TA report. In the next chapter, we discuss some variations in TA.

# 6

## VARIATIONS ON THE METHOD

The flexibility of reflexive thematic analysis (TA) means that there are many variations in how it is applied. In Chapter 2, we outlined this flexibility—how a variety of research questions, epistemological approaches, data collection methods, and data collection formats can all be suitable for TA. These could all be considered variations in how reflexive TA can be used. We also mentioned the various "schools" of TA in Chapter 1, all with different orientations and philosophical underpinnings. While these are not variations of reflexive TA, but rather of TA more broadly, they can make the TA landscape a little murky at times (although this is improving). In the first part of this chapter, we offer examples of what projects from the other schools of TA might look like (one codebook, one coding reliability); here, we identify how the projects discussed differ from reflexive TA. In the second part, we move to variations within reflexive TA, where variation is created by different theoretical orientations to the data, even as the procedures and core values remain the same. We look at three different versions of reflexive TA (one realist, one relativist, and one thematic discourse analysis), in which you would expect to see all the phases we have described in this book play out.

https://doi.org/10.1037/0000238-006
*Essentials of Thematic Analysis*, by G. Terry and N. Hayfield

## VARIATIONS ON TA (THE OTHER "SCHOOLS" OF TA)

### Coding Reliability TA

As we discussed in Chapter 1, coding reliability forms of TA are what might be considered only partially qualitative—because they are primarily answerable to quantitative concerns. This approach often contains concerns about reliability, bias, and replicability and advocates for a realist ontology. Coding reliability will generally use a codebook to establish a constrained number of codes, agreed on early in analysis, and use consensus coding between two or more researchers to ensure analysis is as close to a version of the "truth" of analysis as possible (Joffe, 2012). The following is a discussion of an example paper using a coding reliability form of TA.

In "Stigma in Science: The Case of Earthquake Prediction," Joffe et al. (2018) sought to explore how scientists conceptualize earthquake prediction. They conducted semistructured interviews with 17 earthquake scientists, transcribing them and analyzing them "thematically" (emphasizing prevalence in their definition of TA). In contrast to the organic processes of reflexive TA, they developed a coding frame based on reading the transcripts (a form of familiarization) and deriving a series of codes and their definitions. Two independent coders then tested this coding frame on four randomly selected interviews. Agreement between reviewers was "substantial" (p. 86), producing a Cohen's kappa score of .71, and a frequency table was generated to identify the most prevalent codes. This version of TA shares little in common with reflexive TA as described by Braun and Clarke (e.g., 2006, 2012, 2013, 2019a), with the output closer to domain summaries than the types of themes that reflexive TA might produce: Earthquake prediction is (a) impossible, (b) harmful, and (c) stigmatized. There is no reason why someone within a postpositivist, realist orientation to research should not use this version of TA, but it is not reflexive TA and needs to be treated as independent of the approach we have described in this text.

### Codebook TA

Codebook TA comes with a lot more diversity than coding reliability versions. Codebook versions of TA sit somewhere between reflexive and coding reliability versions of TA. They are qualitative in orientation and philosophy but still seem answerable to quantitative concerns—particularly in the structuring of the coding process. Those who use this approach set up a codebook, often with definitions agreed on by the researchers, using only a small number of the total transcripts, and then apply these codes deductively to the rest of the data corpus. These processes are typically done in the name of "rigor." Often, themes are developed early in the process, in what we would think of as the familiarization phase. The following is a discussion of an example paper using a codebook form of TA.

In "How Can Tomorrow's Doctors Be More Caring? A Phenomenological Investigation," Gillespie et al. (2018) explored the ways patients' experiences of doctors' care could be used in doctors' learning. They took a phenomenological approach and interviewed 10 patients using semistructured interviews, transcribed these interviews verbatim, and then applied template analysis. Their process involved two authors reading all the transcripts and then immediately developing preliminary themes, which formed the basis of the initial template they would use for the rest of the process (the codebook). They then open coded around half of the transcripts to "test" their template, using this process to revise the template. At this point, their themes were relatively well developed and were then used to analyze the remaining transcripts. Their themes were a mix of domain summary (individuality, engagement) and something closer to a multifaceted theme (little things that went above and beyond). As can be seen, this process and often its outputs are quite different from those described in this text.

## VARIATIONS OF REFLEXIVE TA

In Chapter 1, we highlighted that choices need to be made about the theoretical orientation within which you will use reflexive TA. These choices have real effects on the way you might think about the data you are analyzing, with the examples illustrating these differences. Please note that these only reflect three possible variations—there are a lot more that are possible! The first example takes a relatively straightforward realist theoretical position in relation to the data, the other a relativist theoretical expression. The third example, while also using a relativist ontology, takes the principles of reflexive TA and extends these to generate a thematic discourse analysis. We highlight how researchers have used these variations of TA when analyzing their data.

### Realist TA

For many researchers, taking a *realist* position in relation to the worlds of participants and therefore treating their descriptions as transparent reflections of these realities is important (or assumed). Researchers taking a realist approach do not necessarily rely only on semantic coding (see Chapter 3) or claim to be postpositivist (see Chapter 1), but do treat the data and their participants in a particular way. Some phenomenological approaches, for instance, treat the experience and lifeworld of the participant as a real thing that can be accessed through their words (Madill et al., 2018). Rather than treating this approach to data as assumed, or "normal," in reflexive TA, how the data are treated is one option among many for analysis. Postpositivist, some constructivist, and some radical research would align with this particular framing of their participants. The same six-phase approach we have described in previous chapters remains the same, but the interpretative lens creates a specific kind of engagement with the data—a focus on rich description of participants' accounts. The following is a discussion of an example paper using a realist version of reflexive TA.

In "'I Feel Like Everyone Does It'—Adolescents' Perceptions and Awareness of the Association Between Humour, Banter, and Cyberbullying," Steer et al. (2020) explored how young people understood the relationship between bullying and humor in the United Kingdom to help understand motivations to cyberbully. They ran focus groups with 28 students aged 11 to 15 years and transcribed the data verbatim. They used reflexive TA to analyze the data inductively, with one analyst familiarizing themselves with the data, coding the data semantically, and then generating three themes that spoke to the ways that banter and bullying were often hard to distinguish from one another.

While they did not use the term *realist* in their descriptions, a realist position was evident in the language used and the ways interpretation was framed. In other words, the interpretations were generated from connections and congruence between the different participants' talk (rather than through theory) and keeping their interpretations as close to participant concerns and orientations as possible. This does not mean that their analysis was atheoretical; on the contrary, they assumed a lot about the transparency of language and how language can give access to the thoughts of participants. The themes they produced were framed in terms of finding potential avenues to disrupt or mitigate the experience of cyberbullying for young people. They also provided insight into the ways the definitions of cyberbullying may need to be more clearly operationalized.

## Relativist TA

In a *relativist* position, knowledge and meaning are constructed as people engage with the world. The idea of a "real" world is not central to this position, as an external thing that can be "discovered." The researcher interprets the participants' words as producing and reproducing particular realities within the speaker's and hearer's culture. In this perspective, language does not mirror reality but constructs it. Taken-for-granted ideas about the world are not assumed to be "truth" but are instead interrogated and challenged as historically and culturally bound. This position would fit quite closely with most critical, some radical, and all poststructuralist approaches. Coding could be both semantic and latent (see Chapter 3), but the semantic codes are used to inform strongly latent themes, with an emphasis on interpretation rather than description. However, although the interpretation is theoretically informed, it still needs to remain grounded in the data, viewing these data as providing access to the social resources we use to make sense of our worlds. The following is a discussion of an example paper using a relativist version of reflexive TA.

For their paper "Coping by Doping? A Qualitative Inquiry Into Permitted and Prohibited Substance Use in Competitive Rugby," Didymus and Backhouse (2020), in a UK-based study, interviewed 11 participants (three women, eight men) who were competing in rugby league or rugby union at elite levels. They were interested in how players used permitted and prohibited substances to manage the impacts of physical and psychological stress in their sport. In the methods, the researchers identified their relativist ontology and social constructionist epistemology as informing their research. They strongly emphasized the place of reflexivity in their interpretations and spoke of conversations with "critical friends" (see Chapter 3) to help ensure their interpretations were resonating. They chose to analyze the data inductively and deductively in a recursive fashion, with the latter being explicitly informed by a theoretical framework. They gave clear detail about their use of the six phases of reflexive TA, with a long period of familiarization, latent coding, and the development of multiple candidate themes that they then discussed with their critical friends. They explored multiple iterations of theme definitions and names. Instead of treating the player accounts at face value, they highlighted how players would make sense of their experiences in the context of the interviews and identified rhetorical strategies for explaining the use of substances. They also identified how sport cultures produce some effects players need to deal with and are therefore complicit in activities that they simultaneously try to regulate against.

## Thematic Discourse Analysis

Some variations extend reflexive TA rather than simply being about a different theoretical perspective. Researchers have combined TA with discourse analysis to produce *thematic discourse analysis* (TDA), which can sometimes be otherwise referred to as a critical thematic analysis (see Clarke & Braun, 2014; Clarke et al., 2015). This variation is similar to reflexive TA in the development of codes and themes but varies in also moving to identify discourses. Because identification of discourses tends to rely on more conceptual, deeper levels of interpretation than other versions of reflexive TA, codes used in this approach are often latent, and TA practitioners may be more focused on a deductive style of analysis where existing theories or specific frameworks are used to inform what is of interest when analyzing the data. Those who use TDA tend to do so within a poststructuralist framework and may also draw on discursive psychology and how patterns of language play a role in the production of meaning (Clarke & Braun, 2014). Do note, however, that not every author who defines their analysis as TDA necessarily draws on Braun and Clarke's TA; hence, there are also variations of TDA as a form of analysis (e.g., Moran & Lee, 2018; Staneva et al., 2018). The following is a discussion of an example paper using thematic discourse analysis.

For their paper "'We Were Totally Supportive, Of Course': How People Talk About Supporting a Significant Other to Stop or Reduce Their Drinking," Bartram et al. (2019) conducted semistructured interviews with 13 adults in Australia who had "a partner, close friend, or family member who had recently stopped or substantially reduced their alcohol consumption" (p. 1122), with the aim of exploring how support for significant others was accounted for. The researchers took a social constructionist approach and drew on discourse analysis and positioning theory. Discourse analysts focus on how talk can be understood to be not only descriptive but also functional (e.g., how people talk or how text is written can serve to achieve particular ends). Positioning theory relates to how people take up particular identities and social roles through their talk in relation to themselves and others. These theories are used for identifying discourses, the cultural resources that shape how we understand the world, and how people take these up and the roles they produce as a consequence.

Early engagement with the data followed reflexive TA guidelines. The first phase was to read and reread the interview transcripts—in this case with a focus on identifying where participants accounted for (a lack of) support of others' reduction in drinking so that the data included were the most relevant to their research question. The second phase was to code these data extracts. The third phase involved collating codes into themes and an initial thematic structure—again with a focus on how participants and others were positioned in the interview data. In the fourth phase, the initial thematic structure was reviewed and developed. During the fifth phase, further literature review contributed to refining and naming the themes. The final report was akin to discourse analysis and reported three forms of account (deontological, consequentialist, relational). While the procedures followed were based on TA, the authors' theoretical frameworks (discourse analysis, positioning theory) informed the focus and style of the final TDA results.

In this chapter, we looked at two forms of variation of TA. We first discussed the way TA might look if done from a coding reliability or codebook approach (different school approach), which contain different procedures and a fixed theoretical perspective. Second, we talked about how some of the important researcher choices we described in Chapter 1 can differently shape reflexive TA—in particular, creating variations in how analysis proceeds and the types of outputs that can arise (different theoretical framework approach). We provided examples of these different manifestations of TA found in published work to highlight the ways these different approaches might look.

# 7 SUMMARY AND CONCLUSIONS

In this text, we explored the approach to thematic analysis (TA) developed by Virginia Braun and Victoria Clarke, recently referred to as *reflexive TA* (Braun et al., 2018, 2019). We used real data examples from our research to describe the approach in some detail, emphasizing its core characteristics of theoretical flexibility, a focus on ever-increasing and rigorous engagement with data, an emphasis on the researcher reflexivity, and the production of multifaceted, conceptual, meaning-based patterns (themes). It is important to note that these core characteristics of reflexive TA work to provide a rigorous and systematic approach to qualitative data analysis. We also discussed the six phases of reflexive TA as recursive and iterative. This means that reflexive TA was designed not as a strict recipe or rule book but rather as an approach to doing qualitative research qualitatively (Kidder & Fine, 1987; Terry et al., 2017).

Reflexive TA was designed this way explicitly (Braun et al., 2019), and its ongoing evolution and practice should reflect these concerns. As we have (hopefully) made clear, we advocate for this approach to TA, but it is not suited for everyone. In fact, as Victoria Clarke recently commented, "Ironically, the best outcome would be for fewer people to use our approach, because it is not the approach they need, they need something else" (Braun et al., 2019, p. 6).

https://doi.org/10.1037/0000238-007
*Essentials of Thematic Analysis*, by G. Terry and N. Hayfield

Victoria's point is that although it is extremely flexible, reflexive TA cannot be the perfect analytical tool always and everywhere. This is especially true when people need something less flexible and more aligned with their theoretical perspective (as can be the case with grounded theory or interpretive phenomenological analysis), their supervisors' or mentors' methodological knowledge, and the requirements of their research questions. Taking up reflexive TA should be because researchers are convinced of its merits, not because of ideas about its "ease of use" and especially its popularity!

The core values of the method are its main strength; they ensure it is theoretically flexible (rather than atheoretical) while ensuring rigor and guidance that give researchers with a broad range of experience and expertise value. It tends to be misunderstandings about where the method fits within the constellation of qualitative approaches and tools and blurring with other methods and approaches that limit success with it. A recent informal analysis of papers citing Braun and Clarke (2006) indicates that many people do not follow the advice offered in the corpus of writing about reflexive TA. This analysis suggests that many of these writings fall into three categories that are relatively problematic in terms of the existing advice about how to use reflexive TA:

- those simply claiming the approach to justify a vaguely thematic orientation to analysis, with no real procedural information and a tendency to claim themes "emerged" (in reflexive TA, there is the recognition that the researcher actively constructs the themes);

- those providing a basic demonstration of the method but with layers of unnecessary or even inappropriate "enhancements" (e.g., theme frequency counts, interrater scores, codebooks), which often seem to have been "suggested" by (probably well-meaning) supervisors, editors, or reviewers or imposed through uncritical use of tools such as the consolidated criteria for reporting qualitative research (in reflexive TA, trying to standardize how the data are analyzed by different researchers overlooks the way each researcher brings their own unique perspective to the data); or

- a hybrid of both of these, where the constellation of different qualitative methods, methodologies, and worldviews has not been successfully navigated, resulting in an incongruent hodgepodge of citations and processes.

These issues are often compounded by a recent trend toward method proliferation in the social sciences, which can help provide more tools for researchers to use but sometimes risks adding to the confusion for new researchers. This kind of practice involves academics making "extensions," "additions," or "add-ons" to a well-established method with various justifications (often to better fit a method to a particular theoretical lens—typically a [post]positivist one). In the case of reflexive TA, this has often meant citing Braun and Clarke (2006) with no acknowledgment of the corpus of writing since that article, nor (often) a clear understanding of the method itself, especially its core characteristics, such as the need for reflexivity or its flexibility, and therefore the requirement for researchers to make various choices and articulate these. The additions typically involve tweaking some feature of the method, such as redefining its use for certain kinds of text or by adding elements of codebook or coding reliability versions of TA into the mix (see Nowell et al., 2017, for an example of uncritically blending template analysis with the phases of reflexive TA).

We highlight these sorts of additions and method blurring as problematic, not least because we understand how confusing they are for the novice researcher. We argue that a lot more care should be taken by editors and peer reviewers in ensuring that these kinds of additions add value to a method's development. We strongly encourage those using reflexive TA to hold the line! Do not give in to pressure to take on board these components. We understand that this can be hard to do, especially when there are such significant power issues at play, so find critical readers and other supportive people who can help you resist changes you know are incongruent with reflexive TA. The examples given in Chapter 6 should give you some further clarity on where some of these misconceptions exist. Further, we are not suggesting that reflexive thematic analysis is the only way to develop themes from qualitative data, nor that there is no room for its evolution, but emphasize (as we have throughout this text) that understanding the approach you are using or referring to is best research practice. This will help guide you through at least some of the potential pitfalls described earlier.

Reflexive TA does have some limitations. It was designed for identifying patterns across a data set (a horizontal method) and not designed with idiographic analyses (within-case or "vertical" methods) in mind, nor for close reading of texts on its own (where conversation analytical or discursive psychology tools would be more beneficial—see Hepburn and Potter, this series). When these components are core to your design (e.g., because you are taking a phenomenological perspective or drawing on discursive psychology), you will need methods and theoretical frameworks appropriate to the task. While reflexive TA might offer value in an initial analysis of the data set, other approaches might be used to inform later analysis or extend the analytical take. As we discussed in Chapter 6 and some of our research-based examples, there are forms of methodological pluralism and method combinations that do make sense and add value to reflexive TA (e.g., thematic discourse analysis or using insights from critical discursive psychology to extend interpretation), but knowing which of these to use (and when) is a craft skill in itself (see Kahlke, 2014).

We are invested in making the journey using reflexive TA (and other qualitative methods) as straightforward as possible. We are equally keen on supporting people's use of the best methods appropriate to their work and helping them be sufficiently resourced. Much of our support for colleagues and students involves pointing them toward good resources and helping them navigate the potential pitfalls of assuming all qualitative research fits within one theoretical perspective or "paradigm." Our work with Virginia Braun and Victoria Clarke has highlighted just how common this is. Consequently, there is now a well-established corpus of writing produced by Braun, Clarke, and their colleagues related to reflexive TA and situating it in relation to qualitative research more generally. There are also web-based resources, including a companion website supporting their text *Successful Qualitative Research* (Braun & Clarke, 2013; https://studysites.sagepub.com/braunandclarke/) and one devoted to resourcing reflexive TA (https://www.psych.auckland. ac.nz/en/about/thematic-analysis.html). Whichever method or methodology you use, understanding it in depth and not treating methodological understanding as an optional extra is a key component of doing research well.

*Appendix*

# EXEMPLAR STUDIES

Example of a realist approach to analysis:

Williams, A. M., Christopher, G., & Jenkinson, E. (2019). The psychological impact of dependency in adults with chronic fatigue syndrome/myalgic encephalomyelitis: A qualitative exploration. *Journal of Health Psychology, 24*(2), 264–275. https://doi.org/10.1177/1359105316643376

Example of a social constructionist/relativist thematic discourse analysis (variation on thematic analysis):

Wigginton, B., Harris, M. L., Loxton, D., Herbert, D., & Lucke, J. (2015). The feminisation of contraceptive use: Australian women's accounts of accessing contraception. *Feminism & Psychology, 25*(2), 178–198. https://doi.org/10.1177/0959353514562802

Example of a survey study:

Terry, G., & Braun, V. (2016). "I think gorilla-like back effusions of hair are rather a turn-off": 'Excessive hair' and male body hair (removal) discourse. *Body Image, 17*, 14–24. https://doi.org/10.1016/j.bodyim.2016.01.006

Example of an interview study:

Hayfield, N., Terry, G., Clarke, V., & Ellis, S. J. (2019). "Never say never?": Heterosexual, bisexual, and lesbian women's accounts of being childfree. *Psychology of Women Quarterly, 43*(4), 526–538. https://doi.org/10.1177/0361684319863414

Example of a story completion study:

Clarke, V., & Braun, V. (2019). How can a heterosexual man remove his body hair and retain his masculinity? Mapping stories of male body hair depilation. *Qualitative Research in Psychology, 16*(1), 96–114. https://doi.org/10.1080/14780887.2018.1536388

# References

Attard, A., & Coulson, N. S. (2012). A thematic analysis of patient communication in Parkinson's disease online support group discussion forums. *Computers in Human Behavior, 28*(2), 500–506. https://doi.org/10.1016/j.chb.2011.10.022

Barbour, R. S. (2001). Checklists for improving rigour in qualitative research: A case of the tail wagging the dog? *BMJ (Clinical Research Ed.), 322*(7294), 1115–1117. https://doi.org/10.1136/bmj.322.7294.1115

Bartram, A., Crabb, S., Hanson-Easey, S., & Eliott, J. (2019). "We were totally supportive, of course": How people talk about supporting a significant other to stop or reduce their drinking. *Qualitative Health Research, 29*(8), 1120–1131. https://doi.org/10.1177/1049732318809945

Bartram, A., Eliott, J., & Crabb, S. (2017). "Why can't I just not drink?": A qualitative study of adults' social experiences of stopping or reducing alcohol consumption. *Drug and Alcohol Review, 36*(4), 449–455. https://doi.org/10.1111/dar.12461

Bird, C. M. (2005). How I stopped dreading and learned to love transcription. *Qualitative Inquiry, 11*(2), 226–248. https://doi.org/10.1177/1077800404273413

Boyatzis, R. (1998). *Transforming qualitative information: Thematic analysis and code development.* SAGE.

Braun, V., & Clarke, V. (2006). Using thematic analysis in psychology. *Qualitative Research in Psychology, 3*(2), 77–101. https://doi.org/10.1191/1478088706qp063oa

Braun, V., & Clarke, V. (2012). Thematic analysis. In H. Cooper, P. M. Camic, D. L. Long, A. T. Panter, D. Rindskopf, & K. J. Sher (Eds.), *APA handbook of research methods in psychology: Vol. 2. Research designs: Quantitative, qualitative, neuropsychological, and biological* (pp. 57–71). American Psychological Association. https://doi.org/10.1037/13620-004

Braun, V., & Clarke, V. (2013). *Successful qualitative research: A practical guide for beginners.* SAGE.

Braun, V., & Clarke, V. (2016). (Mis)conceptualising themes, thematic analysis, and other problems with Fugard and Potts' (2015) sample-size tool for thematic analysis. *International Journal of Social Research Methodology, 19*(6), 739–743. https://doi.org/10.1080/13645579.2016.1195588

Braun, V., & Clarke, V. (2019a). Reflecting on reflexive thematic analysis. *Qualitative Research in Sport, Exercise and Health, 11*(4), 589–597. https://doi.org/10.1080/2159676X.2019.1628806

Braun, V., & Clarke, V. (2019b). To saturate or not to saturate? Questioning data saturation as a useful concept for thematic analysis and sample-size rationales. *Qualitative Research in Sport, Exercise and Health.* Advance online publication. https://doi.org/10.1080/2159676X.2019.1704846

Braun, V., & Clarke, V. (2020). One size fits all? What counts as quality practice in (reflexive) thematic analysis? *Qualitative Research in Psychology.* Advance online publication. https://doi.org/10.1080/14780887.2020.1769238

Braun, V., Clarke, V., & Gray, D. (Eds.). (2017). *Collecting qualitative data: A practical guide to textual, media and virtual techniques.* Cambridge University Press. https://doi.org/10.1017/9781107295094

Braun, V., Clarke, V., & Hayfield, N. (2019). 'A starting point for your journey, not a map': Nikki Hayfield in conversation with Virginia Braun and Victoria Clarke about thematic analysis. Advance online publication. *Qualitative Research in Psychology.* https://doi.org/10.1080/14780887.2019.1670765

Braun, V., Clarke, V., Hayfield, N., & Terry, G. (2018). Thematic analysis. In P. Liamputtong (Ed.), *Handbook of research methods in health social sciences* (pp. 1–18). Springer. https://doi.org/10.1007/978-981-10-2779-6_103-1

Braun, V., Clarke, V., & Terry, G. (2015). Thematic analysis. In P. Rohleder & A. Lyons (Eds.), *Qualitative research in clinical and health psychology* (pp. 95–113). Palgrave Macmillan.

Braun, V., Tricklebank, G., & Clarke, V. (2013). "It shouldn't stick out from your bikini at the beach": Meaning, gender, and the hairy/hairless body. *Psychology of Women Quarterly, 37*(4), 478–493. https://doi.org/10.1177/0361684313492950

Breakwell, G. M. (2012). Interviewing. In G. M. Breakwell, J. A. Smith, & D. B. Wright (Eds.), *Research methods in psychology* (4th ed., pp. 367–390). SAGE.

Brinkmann, S. (2013). *Qualitative interviewing.* Oxford University Press. https://doi.org/10.1093/acprof:osobl/9780199861392.001.0001

Brinkmann, S., & Kvale, S. (2015). *InterViews: Learning the craft of qualitative research interviewing* (3rd ed.). SAGE.

Brinkmann, S., & Kvale, S. (2017). Ethics in qualitative psychological research. In C. Willig & W. Stainton-Rogers (Eds.), *The SAGE handbook of qualitative research in psychology* (2nd ed., pp. 259–273). SAGE. https://doi.org/10.4135/9781526405555

Brown, T. (2008). Design thinking. *Harvard Business Review, 86*(6), 84–92.

Buetow, S. (2010). Thematic analysis and its reconceptualization as 'saliency analysis.' *Journal of Health Services Research & Policy, 15*(2), 123–125. https://doi.org/10.1258/jhsrp.2009.009081

Clarke, V., & Braun, V. (2014). Thematic analysis. In T. Teo (Ed.), *Encyclopedia of critical psychology* (pp. 1947–1952). Springer. https://doi.org/10.1007/978-1-4614-5583-7_311

Clarke, V., Braun, V., Frith, H., & Moller, N. (2019). Editorial introduction to the special issue: Using story completion methods in qualitative research. *Qualitative Research in Psychology, 16*(1), 1–20. https://doi.org/10.1080/14780887. 2018.1536378

Clarke, V., Braun, V., & Hayfield, N. (2015). Thematic analysis. In J. Smith (Ed.), *Qualitative psychology: A practical guide to research methods* (3rd ed., pp. 222–248). SAGE.

Clarke, V., Hayfield, N., Moller, N., Tischner, I., & the Story Completion Research Group. (2017). Once upon a time . . . qualitative story completion methods. In V. Braun, V. Clarke, & D. Gray (Eds.), *Collecting qualitative data: A practical guide to textual, media and virtual techniques* (pp. 45–70). Cambridge University Press. https://doi.org/10.1017/9781107295094.004

Didymus, F. F., & Backhouse, S. H. (2020). Coping by doping? A qualitative inquiry into permitted and prohibited substance use in competitive rugby. *Psychology of Sport and Exercise, 49*, 101680. https://doi.org/10.1016/j.psychsport.2020. 101680

Eatough, V., & Smith, J. (2017). Interpretative phenomenological analysis. In C. Willig & W. Stainton-Rogers (Eds.), *The SAGE handbook of qualitative research in psychology* (pp. 193–209). SAGE. https://doi.org/10.4135/ 9781526405555.n12

Elliott, R., Fischer, C. T., & Rennie, D. L. (1999). Evolving guidelines for publication of qualitative research studies in psychology and related fields. *British Journal of Clinical Psychology, 38*(3), 215–229. https://doi.org/10.1348/ 014466599162782

Finlay, L., & Gough, B. (Eds.). (2003). *Reflexivity: A practical guide for researchers in health and social sciences.* Blackwell Science. https://doi.org/10.1002/ 9780470776094

Flick, U. (2018). *An introduction to qualitative research* (6th ed.). SAGE.

Gillespie, H., Kelly, M., Gormley, G., King, N., Gilliland, D., & Dornan, T. (2018). How can tomorrow's doctors be more caring? A phenomenological investigation. *Medical Education, 52*(10), 1052–1063. https://doi.org/10.1111/ medu.13684

Grant, B. M., & Giddings, L. S. (2002). Making sense of methodologies: A paradigm framework for the novice researcher. *Contemporary Nurse, 13*(1), 10–28. https://doi.org/10.5172/conu.13.1.10

Gray, D., Royall, B., & Malson, H. (2017). Hypothetically speaking: Using vignettes as a standalone qualitative method. In V. Braun, V. Clarke, & D. Gray (Eds.), *Collecting qualitative data: A practical guide to textual, media and virtual techniques* (pp. 71–93). Cambridge University Press. https://doi.org/ 10.1017/9781107295094.005

Guest, G., MacQueen, K., & Namey, E. (2012). *Applied thematic analysis.* SAGE. Advance online publication. https://doi.org/10.4135/9781483384436

Hanna, P. (2012). Using internet technologies (such as Skype) as a research medium: A research note. *Qualitative Research, 12*(2), 239–242. https://doi.org/ 10.1177/1468794111426607

Hanna, P., & Mwale, S. (2017). I'm not with you, yet I am. In V. Braun, V. Clarke, & D. Gray (Eds.), *Collecting qualitative data: A practical guide to textual, media and virtual techniques* (pp. 235–255). Cambridge University Press. https://doi.org/10.1017/9781107295094.013

Hayfield, N., & Huxley, C. (2015). Insider and outsider perspectives: Reflections on researcher identities in research with lesbian and bisexual women. *Qualitative Research in Psychology, 12*(2), 91–106. https://doi.org/10.1080/14780887.2014.918224

Hayfield, N., Terry, G., Clarke, V., & Ellis, S. J. (2019). "Never say never?": Heterosexual, bisexual, and lesbian women's accounts of being childfree. *Psychology of Women Quarterly, 43*(4), 526–538. https://doi.org/10.1177/0361684319863414

Hegarty, R. S., Treharne, G. J., Stebbings, S., Graham, K., & Conner, T. S. (2019). Optimising daily diary questionnaires about fatigue, psychological flexibility and well-being: Perspectives of people with rheumatic disease. *Psychology & Health, 34*(2), 181–199. https://doi.org/10.1080/08870446.2018.1520232

Hsieh, H.-F., & Shannon, S. (2005). Three approaches to qualitative content analysis. *Qualitative Health Research, 15*(9), 1277–1288. https://doi.org/10.1177/1049732305276687

Humble, Á., & Radina, M. (2019). *How qualitative data analysis happens: Moving beyond "themes emerged."* Routledge.

Isaacs, D. H. (2016). Social representations of intimate partner violence in the South African media. *South African Journal of Psychology, 46*(4), 491–503. https://doi.org/10.1177/0081246316628815

Jankowski, G. S., Fawkner, H., Slater, A., & Tiggemann, M. (2014). "Appearance potent"? A content analysis of UK gay and straight men's magazines. *Body Image, 11*(4), 474–481. https://doi.org/10.1016/j.bodyim.2014.07.010

Jennings, E., Braun, V., & Clarke, V. (2019). Breaking gendered boundaries? Exploring constructions of counter-normative body hair practices in Aotearoa/New Zealand using story completion. *Qualitative Research in Psychology, 16*(1), 74–95. https://doi.org/10.1080/14780887.2018.1536386

Joffe, H. (2012). Thematic analysis. In D. Harper & A. R. Thompson (Eds.), *Qualitative methods in mental health and psychotherapy: A guide for students and practitioners* (pp. 209–223). Wiley. https://doi.org/10.1002/9781119973249.ch15

Joffe, H., Rossetto, T., Bradley, C., & O'Connor, C. (2018). Stigma in science: The case of earthquake prediction. *Disasters, 42*(1), 81–100. https://doi.org/10.1111/disa.12237

Jowett, A., & Peel, E. (2009). Chronic illness in non-heterosexual contexts: An online survey of experiences. *Feminism & Psychology, 19*(4), 454–474. https://doi.org/10.1177/0959353509342770

Jowett, A., Peel, E., & Shaw, R. L. (2012). Sex and diabetes: A thematic analysis of gay and bisexual men's accounts. *Journal of Health Psychology, 17*(3), 409–418. https://doi.org/10.1177/1359105311412838

Kahlke, R. M. (2014). Generic qualitative approaches: Pitfalls and benefits of methodological mixology. *International Journal of Qualitative Methods, 13*(1), 37–52. https://doi.org/10.1177/160940691401300119

Kidder, L., & Fine, M. (1987). Qualitative and quantitative methods: When stories converge. *New Directions for Program Evaluation, 1987*(35), 57–75. https://doi.org/10.1002/ev.1459

King, N. (2012). Doing template analysis. In G. Symon & C. Cassell (Eds.), *Qualitative organizational research: Core methods and current challenges* (pp. 426–450). SAGE. https://doi.org/10.4135/9781526435620.n24

Levitt, H. M., Bamberg, M., Creswell, J. W., Frost, D. M., Josselson, R., & Suárez-Orozco, C. (2018). Journal article reporting standards for qualitative primary, qualitative meta-analytic, and mixed methods research in psychology: The APA Publications and Communications Board task force report. *American Psychologist, 73*(1), 26–46. https://doi.org/10.1037/amp0000151

Levitt, H. M., Motulsky, S. L., Wertz, F. J., Morrow, S. L., & Ponterotto, J. G. (2017). Recommendations for designing and reviewing qualitative research in psychology: Promoting methodological integrity. *Qualitative Psychology, 4*(1), 2–22. https://doi.org/10.1037/qup0000082

Lincoln, Y. S., & Guba, E. G. (1985). *Naturalistic inquiry.* SAGE. https://doi.org/10.1016/0147-1767(85)90062-8

Lunde, C., & Gattario, K. H. (2017). Performance or appearance? Young female sport participants' body negotiations. *Body Image, 21*, 81–89. https://doi.org/10.1016/j.bodyim.2017.03.001

Madill, A., Flowers, P., Frost, N., & Locke, A. (2018). A meta-methodology to enhance pluralist qualitative research: One man's use of socio-sexual media and midlife adjustment to HIV. *Psychology & Health, 33*(10), 1209–1228. https://doi.org/10.1080/08870446.2018.1475670

Madill, A., & Gough, B. (2008). Qualitative research and its place in psychological science. *Psychological Methods, 13*(3), 254–271. https://doi.org/10.1037/a0013220

Merton, R. (1975). Thematic analysis in science: Notes on Holton's concept. *Science, 188*(4186), 335–338. https://doi.org/10.1126/science.188.4186.335

Miles, M., & Huberman, A. (1994). *Qualitative data analysis: An expanded sourcebook.* SAGE.

Millward, L. (2012). Focus groups. In G. M. Breakwell, J. A. Smith, & D. B. Wright, *Research methods in psychology* (4th ed., pp. 411–437). SAGE.

Moran, C., & Lee, C. (2018). 'Everyone wants a vagina that looks less like a vagina': Australian women's views on dissatisfaction with genital appearance. *Journal of Health Psychology, 23*(2), 229–239. https://doi.org/10.1177/1359105316637588

Moskowitz, D. A., Turrubiates, J., Lozano, H., & Hajek, C. (2013). Physical, behavioral, and psychological traits of gay men identifying as bears. *Archives of Sexual Behavior, 42*(5), 775–784. https://doi.org/10.1007/s10508-013-0095-z

Nicholas, H., & McDowall, A. (2012). When work keeps us apart: A thematic analysis of the experience of business travellers. *Community Work & Family*, *15*(3), 335–355. https://doi.org/10.1080/13668803.2012.668346

Nicholls, D. (2009). Qualitative research: Part three—Methods. *International Journal of Therapy and Rehabilitation*, *16*(12), 638–647. https://doi.org/10.12968/ijtr.2009.16.12.45433

Novick, G. (2008). Is there a bias against telephone interviews in qualitative research? *Research in Nursing & Health*, *31*(4), 391–398. https://doi.org/10.1002/nur.20259

Nowell, L. S., Norris, J. M., White, D. E., & Moules, N. J. (2017). Thematic analysis: Striving to meet the trustworthiness criteria. *International Journal of Qualitative Methods*. https://doi.org/10.1177/1609406917733847

Opperman, E., Braun, V., Clarke, V., & Rogers, C. (2014). "It feels so good it almost hurts": Young adults' experiences of orgasm and sexual pleasure. *Journal of Sex Research*, *51*(5), 503–515. https://doi.org/10.1080/00224499.2012.753982

Parker, I. (2004). Criteria for qualitative research in psychology. *Qualitative Research in Psychology*, *1*(2), 95–106. https://doi.org/10.1191/1478088704qp010oa

Richards, L. (2014). *Handling qualitative data: A practical guide*. SAGE.

Ritchie, J., & Spencer, L. (1994). Qualitative data analysis for applied policy research. In A. Bryman & R. Burgess (Eds.), *Analysing qualitative data* (pp. 173–194). Taylor & Francis. https://doi.org/10.4324/9780203413081_chapter_9

Sandelowski, M. (1994). Focus on qualitative methods. Notes on transcription. *Research in Nursing & Health*, *17*(4), 311–314. https://doi.org/10.1002/nur.4770170410

Sandelowski, M. (2007). Words that should be seen but not written. *Research in Nursing & Health*, *30*(2), 129–130. https://doi.org/10.1002/nur.20198

Sandelowski, M., & Leeman, J. (2012). Writing usable qualitative health research findings. *Qualitative Health Research*, *22*(10), 1404–1413. https://doi.org/10.1177/1049732312450368

Silverman, D. (2013). *Doing qualitative research* (4th ed.). SAGE.

Sims-Schouten, W., Riley, S. C., & Willig, C. (2007). Critical realism in discourse analysis: A presentation of a systematic method of analysis using women's talk of motherhood, childcare and female employment as an example. *Theory & Psychology*, *17*, 101–124. https://doi.org/10.1177/0959354307073153

Smith, B., & McGannon, K. R. (2018). Developing rigor in qualitative research: Problems and opportunities within sport and exercise psychology. *International Review of Sport and Exercise Psychology*, *11*(1), 101–121. https://doi.org/10.1080/1750984X.2017.1317357

Smith, J., Flowers, P., & Larkin, M. (2009). *Interpretative phenomenological analysis: Theory, method and research*. SAGE.

Smith, J., & Osborne, M. (2003). Interpretative phenomenological analysis. In J. Smith (Ed.), *Qualitative psychology: A practical guide to research methods* (pp. 51–80). SAGE.

Stainton Rogers, W., & Willig, C. (2017). Introduction. In C. Willig & W. Stainton Rogers (Eds.), *The SAGE handbook of qualitative research in psychology* (2nd ed., pp. 1–14). SAGE.

Staneva, A. A., Gibson, A. F., Webb, P. M., & Beesley, V. L. (2018). The imperative for a triumph-over-tragedy story in women's accounts of undergoing chemotherapy for ovarian cancer. *Qualitative Health Research, 28*(11), 1759–1768. https://doi.org/10.1177/1049732318778261

Steer, O. L., Betts, L. R., Baguley, T., & Binder, J. F. (2020). "I feel like everyone does it"—adolescents' perceptions and awareness of the association between humour, banter, and cyberbullying. *Computers in Human Behavior, 108*, 106297. https://doi.org/10.1016/j.chb.2020.106297

Terry, G., & Braun, V. (2016). "I think gorilla-like back effusions of hair are rather a turn-off": 'Excessive hair' and male body hair (removal) discourse. *Body Image, 17*, 14–24. https://doi.org/10.1016/j.bodyim.2016.01.006

Terry, G., & Braun, V. (2017). Short but often sweet: The surprising potential of qualitative survey methods. In V. Braun, V. Clarke, & D. Gray (Eds.), *Collecting qualitative data: A practical guide to textual, media and virtual techniques* (pp. 15–44). Cambridge University Press. https://doi.org/10.1017/9781107295094.003

Terry, G., & Hayfield, N. (2020). Thematic analysis. In M. Ward & S. Delamont (Eds.), *Handbook of qualitative research in education* (2nd ed., pp. 430–441). Edward Elgar Publishing. https://doi.org/10.4337/9781788977159.00049

Terry, G., Hayfield, N., Clarke, V., & Braun, V. (2017). Thematic analysis. In C. Willig & W. Stainton Rogers (Eds.), *The SAGE handbook of qualitative research in psychology* (2nd ed., pp. 17–36). SAGE. https://doi.org/10.4135/9781526405555.n2

Terry, G., & Kayes, N. (2020). Person centered care in neurorehabilitation: A secondary analysis. *Disability and Rehabilitation, 42*(16), 2334–2343. https://doi.org/10.1080/09638288.2018.1561952

Tong, A., Sainsbury, P., & Craig, J. (2007). Consolidated criteria for reporting qualitative research (COREQ): A 32-item checklist for interviews and focus groups. *International Journal for Quality in Health Care, 19*(6), 349–357. https://doi.org/10.1093/intqhc/mzm042

Tracy, S. J. (2010). Qualitative quality: Eight "big-tent" criteria for excellent qualitative research. *Qualitative Inquiry, 16*(10), 837–851. https://doi.org/10.1177/1077800410383121

Ussher, J. M., Sandoval, M., Perz, J., Wong, W. T., & Butow, P. (2013). The gendered construction and experience of difficulties and rewards in cancer care. *Qualitative Health Research, 23*(7), 900–915. https://doi.org/10.1177/1049732313484197

Varpio, L., Ajjawi, R., Monrouxe, L. V., O'Brien, B. C., & Rees, C. E. (2017). Shedding the cobra effect: Problematising thematic emergence, triangulation, saturation and member checking. *Medical Education, 51*(1), 40–50. https://doi.org/10.1111/medu.13124

Wada, M., Clarke, L. H., & Mortenson, W. B. (2019). 'I am busy independent woman who has sense of humor, caring about others': Older adults' self-representations in online dating profiles. *Ageing and Society, 39*(5), 951–976. https://doi.org/10.1017/S0144686X17001325

Williams, A. M., Christopher, G., & Jenkinson, E. (2019). The psychological impact of dependency in adults with chronic fatigue syndrome/myalgic encephalomyelitis: A qualitative exploration. *Journal of Health Psychology, 24*(2), 264–275. https://doi.org/10.1177/1359105316643376

Willig, C. (2013). *Introducing qualitative research in psychology* (3rd ed.). Open University Press.

Yardley, L. (2000). Dilemmas in qualitative health research. *Psychology & Health, 15*(2), 215–228. https://doi.org/10.1080/08870440008400302

# Index

# About the Authors

**Gareth Terry, PhD,** is a senior lecturer in rehabilitation studies at Auckland University of Technology (AUT) in Aotearoa/New Zealand. He works out of the Centre for Person Centred Research (PCR), where he leads the research theme Disability, Diversity and Accessibility in the Centre. He has worked as a health researcher for the past 16 years and is interested in research that explores the intersection of gender, bodies, and health. His work is informed by his background in critical health psychology and, more recently, (post) critical rehabilitation studies, with his current research exploring person centredness in rehabilitation, disability, and how ideas of access enable and constrain certain ways of being and doing in the world. Dr. Terry has written a number of chapters related to qualitative methods, with Virginia Braun, Victoria Clarke, and Nikki Hayfield. He also has a growing interest in research that draws on principles and practices of codesign and its implications for knowledge translation activity. He contributes to a range of projects and provides methodological support to the PCR team and the wider School of Clinical Sciences at AUT.

**Nikki Hayfield, PhD,** began conducting qualitative research as a student at the University of the West of England (UWE), Bristol, where she completed a doctorate in psychology. She is currently a senior lecturer in social psychology and teaches human sexuality and qualitative research methods to undergraduate and postgraduate students, as well as supervising student projects in these areas. Dr. Hayfield's research focuses on qualitative methods, and her areas of expertise are in LGBTQ+ and heterosexual sexualities across the life span, with a particular focus on bisexual and other marginalized identities. She has written journal articles and book chapters on qualitative research methods, including on thematic analysis with Victoria Clarke, Virginia Braun, and Gareth Terry. She has also published qualitative research on experiences, identities, marginalization, relationships, and child freedom in a range of journals (including *Feminism & Psychology*, *Psychology & Sexuality*, and *Psychology of Women Quarterly*). She is currently the leader of the Identities, Subjectivities and Inequalities theme of the Social Sciences Research Group at UWE and is a consulting editor for *Feminism & Psychology*. In 2020, Dr. Hayfield published her book *Bisexual and Pansexual Identities: Exploring and Challenging Invisibility and Invalidation*.

# About the Series Editors

**Clara E. Hill, PhD,** earned her doctorate at Southern Illinois University in 1974. She started her career in 1974 as an assistant professor in the Department of Psychology, University of Maryland, College Park, and is currently there as a professor.

She is the president-elect of the Society for the Advancement of Psychotherapy, and has been the president of the Society for Psychotherapy Research, the editor of the *Journal of Counseling Psychology*, and the editor of *Psychotherapy Research*.

Dr. Hill was awarded the Leona Tyler Award for Lifetime Achievement in Counseling Psychology from Division 17 (Society of Counseling Psychology) and the Distinguished Psychologist Award from Division 29 (Society for the Advancement of Psychotherapy) of the American Psychological Association, the Distinguished Research Career Award from the Society for Psychotherapy Research, and the Outstanding Lifetime Achievement Award from the Section on Counseling and Psychotherapy Process and Outcome Research of the Society of Counseling Psychology. Her major research interests are helping skills, psychotherapy process and outcome, training therapists, dream work, and qualitative research.

She has published more than 250 journal articles, 80 chapters in books, and 17 books (including *Therapist Techniques and Client Outcomes: Eight Cases of Brief Psychotherapy*; *Helping Skills: Facilitating Exploration, Insight, and Action*; and *Dream Work in Therapy: Facilitating Exploration, Insight, and Action*).

**Sarah Knox, PhD,** joined the faculty of Marquette University in 1999 and is a professor in the Department of Counselor Education and Counseling Psychology in the College of Education. She earned her doctorate at the University of Maryland and completed her predoctoral internship at The Ohio State University.

Dr. Knox's research has been published in a number of journals, including *The Counseling Psychologist, Counselling Psychology Quarterly, Journal of Counseling Psychology, Psychotherapy, Psychotherapy Research,* and *Training and Education in Professional Psychology.* Her publications focus on the psychotherapy process and relationship, supervision and training, and qualitative research. She has presented her research both nationally and internationally and has provided workshops on consensual qualitative research at both U.S. and international venues.

She currently serves as coeditor-in-chief of *Counselling Psychology Quarterly* and is also on the publication board of Division 29 (Society for the Advancement of Psychotherapy) of the American Psychological Association. Dr. Knox is a fellow of Division 17 (Society of Counseling Psychology) and Division 29 of the American Psychological Association.